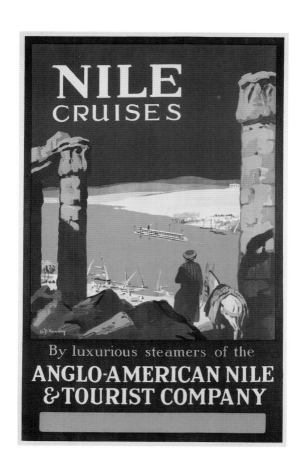

ON THE NILE
IN THE GOLDEN AGE OF TRAVEL

ANDREW HUMPHREYS

The American University in Cairo Press
Cairo New York

PAGE ONE Poster advertising the Anglo-American Nile Company's cruises, circa 1920
PREVIOUS SPREAD Thomas Cook & Son steamers anchored at Aswan, circa 1900
OPPOSITE A Cook & Son's porter, by artist Lance Thackeray

First published in 2021 by
The American University in Cairo Press
113 Sharia Kasr el Aini, Cairo, Egypt
One Rockefeller Plaza, 10th Floor, New York, NY 10020
www.aucpress.com

ISBN 978 1 649 03112 9

Library of Congress Cataloging-in-Publication Data applied for

1 2 3 4 5   25 24 23 22 21

Picture research and design by Gadi Farfour
Photography by Gary Ombler
Color correction by Andrea El-Akshar
Printed in China

CONTENTS

COOKS TOURS
IN
EGYPT,
ARABIA PETRÆA,
AND
LOWER NUBIA.

SCALES
Natural Scale 1:2,854,868 = 45...

Railways
Routes of Cooks To...
Submarine Telegra...
Steamer Routes with...

HOTEL de LONDRES et NEW-YORK
13 et 15, Place du Havre
GARE St-LAZARE

48 Route 4. CAIRO. Street Scenes.

chief'); 'yemînik yâ bint' ('to thy right, girl'); 'dahrik yâ sitt' ('thy back, lady'); 'yâ 'arûsa' ('bride'); 'yâ sherîf' (descendant of the prophet); 'yâ efendi' (the title for a native gentleman).— They endeavour to excite compassion by invoking the aid of Allah: 'yâ Mohannin yâ Rabb' ('O awakener of pity, O Master'); 'tâlib min Allâh hakk lukmet 'eish' ('I seek from my Lord the price of a morsel of bread'). 'ana deif Allâh wa'n-nebi' ('I am the guest of God and of the Prophet'). The usual answer of the passer-by is 'al Allâh', or 'Allâh yehannin 'aleik' ('God will have mercy on thee') or 'Allâh ya'tîk' ('God give thee'; comp. p. xxiv).

The Sakkâ, or water-carrier, with his goatskin of water, carried either by himself or by a donkey, still plies his trade in Cairo, although the water-works supply every house in the city, as well as the public sebîls (p. clxxxii), with water, and though many of the houses there are brass tubes through which passers-by may take a draught from the main pipes. The Hemâli also, who belong to one of the orders of dervishes (p. xci), are engaged in selling water, which they flavour with orange-blossom (zahr), while others use liquorice ('erksûs) or raisins (zebîb). There are also numerous itinerant vendors of fruit, vegetables, and sweetmeats, ... to Europeans usually look very uninviting. The Rammâl or ... by consulting the sand. Lastly, there are itinerant ... squatting by the side of the road, offers to tell the fortune ... tabbâkh), with portable kitchens, who sell ... and other comestibles. ... their shops open to the street ... they may be seen shat...

Street Scenes. CAIRO. 4. Route. 49

Several times during the day and also at night the solemn and sonorous cry of the muezzin, summoning the faithful to prayer (see p. lxxxvii), reverberates from the tops of the minarets (mâdna). When the shops are shut the watchmen (bauwâb) place their beds (serîr) of palm-twigs in the streets outside the entrances and prepare to spend the night there; sometimes they have only mats or rugs to sleep on. The street-traffic ceases in the Arab quarters comparatively early, while in the European districts it goes on till nearly midnight. But during the month of Ramadan it continues throughout the whole ...

HOTEL
LONDRES
& NEW-YO...
PAR...

They do not fail...
to find time for the same
tricks as European school-

MISS RIGGS GOES ABROAD

"The tourists are coming!" WILLIAM HENRY RUSSELL, 1869

Late afternoon on Monday 25 January 1869, Miss Riggs, of Hampstead in north London, left her home and made her way across the city to London Bridge station. There, she met up with eleven others and, together, the party caught the 6:45 p.m. train for Newhaven on the coast, where they boarded a ferry for Dieppe in France.

Once over the Channel, they caught another train on to Paris where they spent the night at the Hôtel Londres et New York, on the place du Havre, across from the Gare St. Lazare. The following day, Miss Riggs and a companion, Miss Porter, visited the Louvre, where they admired Murillo's *Holy Family* and then lost their way trying to get back to the hotel. They found it in time for dinner at six, at which point they were joined by several new additions to the group. And that was it for Paris—at 10:15 p.m. that evening they boarded another train and left the city.

There was a brief halt at Dijon at three in the morning, when they were given soup, but otherwise it was straight on via Macon and Chambery, and up into the Alps on the Mont Cenis Pass Railway. This had only opened the previous year and was the first mountain railway in the world (although it would close just two years later, superseded by a new tunnel railway). There was excitement, and maybe even a little fear, at the difficulty the engine had in hauling the carriages up the steep incline; sometimes the gasping train stopped entirely and teetered on the verge of going backward. At one point it halted under a wooden cover meant to keep snowdrifts off the track and almost choked its passengers with the trapped smoke.

The party arrived in Turin, Italy at 4 a.m. on the 29th, where they slept for just a few hours, at a hotel called the Trombetta, before rising for breakfast at ten and heading out to explore. It was snowing, but that didn't stop Miss Riggs and five companions from enthusiastically ticking off a list of palazzos, piazzas, and churches.

Early the next morning, the party, which by now numbered twenty-seven, was on its way again. There was just one more overnight stop, in

ABOVE The Adriatic and Oriental Company's screw-steamer *Cairo*, sister ship to the *Brindisi*, on which Miss Riggs sailed from Italy to Alexandria

BELOW Miss Riggs's luggage allowance for the trip was a surprisingly modest 60 pounds (27 kg), but she was a little over on account of her saddle

Ancona. It being Sunday, a German minister was found to deliver a service in English, before Miss Riggs and her company, having journeyed overland for almost a week, arrived at their final destination in Europe: the port of Brindisi on Italy's east coast.

It was here, on the shores of the Adriatic, that Miss Riggs began to sense Europe slipping away and an otherness approaching. The town was ancient, with immense walls and narrow streets; its people were dark and Moorish, the men dressed in large hooded cloaks. It looked, she thought, a dangerous place. The party didn't stay long. They lunched at a hotel with sandy floors—and were glad not to be sleeping there—then at five that afternoon clambered into rowboats to be transferred to a steamer of the Adriatic and Oriental Company, which bore the name of its home port. At nine that evening, the *Brindisi* drew anchor and slipped out to sea.

The cabins were small, stuffy, and shared, and so Miss Riggs spent much of her time on deck, reclining in a comfortable cane chair observing the Greek islands passing in the distance. At one point the passengers were entertained by a pair of porpoises playing in the ship's wake. Otherwise Miss Riggs was content to read her copy of *Lloyd's Oriental Guide to Egypt*—Egypt being the Brindisi's destination.

By seven on the morning of 4 February, after three nights at sea, all the party was up on deck. The ship was at rest and there, visible a short distance away, was Alexandria. A flotilla of small boats was already jostling for position beside the *Brindisi*, and over the next hour its passengers and luggage were transferred to those and rowed ashore. Passports were stamped in a small building on the wharf before everyone was settled in carriages and driven through thick mud to the city's main square, where they had lodgings at the Hôtel de l'Europe.

Four days were allowed for sightseeing in Alexandria, which included expeditions to the waterfront palace of Egypt's ruler, His Excellency the Khedive Ismail Pasha, and to an American missionary school. Miss Riggs and a few companions visited Alexandria's lone standing obelisk and admired its hieroglyphs, although in her diary she confuses it with Pompey's Pillar, the Roman-era column that stood over on the other side of the city. She also expressed disappointment at not seeing the library "celebrated by the Ptolemics"—an institution that was burned down over fifteen hundred years previously. Lloyd's guide to Egypt does not seem to have been much of a guide. She was, however, very pleased by the purchase of a pair of smoke-colored spectacles.

On Sunday 7 February, the party took an early train to Cairo, a journey of five hours. On arrival they were transferred by carriage to Shepheard's, the city's best-known hotel, only to find there weren't enough rooms available for everybody. Alternative arrangements were hastily made and some of the travelers were found lodgings at two nearby hotels, the Royal and the Orient. Sightseeing began immediately after lunch, hastened by the knowledge that the party only had two days in Cairo before it would be on the move again; they were due to board two boats that even now were being readied for departure up the Nile. (As the Nile flows north, one sails "up" it to go south.)

In the time allowed, the first item on Miss Riggs's agenda was the medieval Citadel high on a rocky bluff on the eastern edge of the city,

Miss Riggs's first visit in Egypt was to Ismail Pasha's Ras al-Tin Palace at Alexandria, which she found neglected and forlorn, the viceroy and his attendants only using it in summer

On 8 February Miss Riggs stood on the terraces of the Citadel at Cairo to look across the city to the Pyramids at Giza, the pyramids of Saqqara and Dahshur, and "the grand and endless desert"

from where she admired the views back across Cairo to the Pyramids and desert beyond. She and her companions took in the fortress's mosques and descended Joseph's Well, bored 260 feet deep into rock: interesting to go down but exhausting to climb back up. The following morning was spent in the bazaars, which Miss Riggs found "most wonderfully oriental and novel to English people," while the afternoon was taken with visits to several mission schools, where she thought the children had "good foreheads and could be trained for much." The next morning they prepared for departure.

The person responsible for setting such a brisk pace was the tour leader, the enterprising Mr. Thomas Cook. He had been there at London Bridge station to greet and collect his party and had personally escorted them across Europe and the Mediterranean to Egypt. For almost thirty years Cook had been leading tour groups around Great Britain, across Europe, and even farther afield, but this particular trip was something new, the fulfillment of a long-held dream.

Born on 22 November 1808, in the region of Derbyshire in the English Midlands, Thomas Cook was only four when his father died. To help support his mother, he left school at ten and went to work as a gardener's boy on a local estate. Later, he was apprenticed to an uncle who was a wood-turner, but it was when he finished his apprenticeship and took work with a printer of books for the Baptist Association that he found his real calling, that of teenage missionary. He journeyed from village to village, distributing religious tracts and assisting in the setting up of Sunday schools. Although his efforts were concentrated in the counties around Derbyshire, in the year 1829 he still managed, by his own reckoning, to clock up 2,692 miles, most of which was covered on foot—an early introduction to travel. In 1833 he married and the following year saw the birth of a son, with the result that Cook swapped his itinerant lifestyle for a more settled existence with his young family in a small market town, where he returned to living as a wood-turner. Cook directed his evangelical zeal to what was viewed at the time as one of the most serious of all social ills, drunkenness. He became part of a nationwide temperance movement, dedicated to weaning the working classes off their wasteful indulgence in beer and spirits.

Cook's devotion to God's work was matched by an equally firm belief in the virtues of Progress and Industry, and at the age of thirty-three he formed a vision of how this trinity might be combined. On Monday 5 July 1841, Cook arranged for some 570 workers from Leicester to travel on the newly laid railway to Loughborough, a distance of eleven miles, where they would attend a temperance meeting and be entertained by a band.

Further similar excursions followed. Cook wasn't slow to see that these outings could combine social reform with a measure of profit (as Cecil Rhodes would later put it, "Pure philanthropy is very well in its way but *philanthropy plus five percent* is a good deal better"). In the summer of 1845,

On the 9th she visited Cairo's "Turkish bazaars," which she described as "miles of winding narrow streets covered over with matting to protect from the sun"

he led his first professional trip, which was to Liverpool, followed by an outing to Scotland in 1846.

For a few years, trips to the north of Britain were the mainstay of his business, but in 1851 there was money to be made ferrying tourists down to London for the Great Exhibition, the first of the World's Fairs that were to become so popular in the second half of the nineteenth century. He made his first forays across the English Channel to mainland Europe in 1855 and, in 1861, led his first proper trip to Paris. In June 1863, he took his first party—which numbered over sixty tourists—to Switzerland, pushing on into Italy in July 1864 and crossing the Atlantic to America in the spring of 1866.

By the beginning of 1868 Cook claimed to have organized the travel of some two million people. Using the promise of large numbers of sales, Cook secured discounts that were then passed on to his customers, who received the benefit of a single payment covering all travel and transit, with vouchers for hotel accommodation and meals. Perhaps even more significantly, they were also insulated from the complications and risks of local financial transactions.

As well as opening up travel to classes of people who could otherwise never have afforded, or even considered, such a thing—travel for pleasure until this time being the preserve of the idle rich—Cook also altered the perception of travel as a largely male-only pastime. His excursions and tours appealed particularly to women, who felt able to sign up for his tours either alone or with a companion. Cook cannily promoted himself as "the traveling chaperone." The teetotaler who entered the travel business as a form of missionary enterprise had become a pioneer in the concept of mass tourism.

Given his biblical bent, it's no surprise that Cook would eventually turn his attention to Egypt and Palestine. With Europe largely conquered and inroads made into America, he was ready to act on his ambitions. In autumn 1868 he set out for Constantinople, Beirut, Jaffa, Alexandria, and Cairo to investigate transport arrangements, assess hotels, and estimate costs. He had received conflicting information on the suitability of the region for western tourists, so it was essential he reconnoiter the ground alone first: "The reputation of twenty-eight years of tourist management will not be sacrificed for a chimera," he wrote. But his expectation was definitely that the venture would be a success, and he was already promoting and accepting down payments for a proposed group tour a month before setting off on his solo exploratory trip.

An early piece of Thomas Cook marketing collateral from 1865, two years after he led his first party to Switzerland and the year after his entry into Italy

Which brings us back to Cairo, and Miss Riggs and her fellow travelers, who had responded to Cook's advertisements and signed up for his historic inaugural trip. Historic, not because this was the first organized tour to Egypt and Palestine: another English tour operator, Henry Gaze, had recently led three small groups here in advance of Cook.★ And this was hardly virgin territory: London-based publisher John Murray had issued its first guidebook to Egypt as far back as 1847, and even before then, as early as 1843, the British consul in Cairo was complaining about the flood of English tourists. However, within just a few years, the name of Thomas Cook would come to dominate the business of touring Egypt, and particularly of cruising the Nile, a dominance that would last for three-quarters of a century.

Despite the consul's comments, for a European (or American) to journey to Egypt was still sufficiently remarkable that Miss Riggs decided to keep a detailed diary of her trip. Her pocket notebook crammed with

An early Thomas Cook party assembles for the camera in Pompeii in 1868, the same year the pioneering travel leader would make his first exploratory visit to Egypt. He sits front center, the gent with the balding head

★ Born 1825 in London, Henry Gaze was a former bootmaker who set up a travel business in Southampton in 1844. He was offering tours to France and the Continent, including to the battlefield of Waterloo before Cook, and reached Egypt before him, too. The two companies were major rivals through the latter half of the nineteenth century, until Gaze died in 1894, and the business passed to his three sons, who managed to steer it into bankruptcy by 1903. The name of Henry Gaze has long since faded into obscurity, but in his day it was every bit as well known as that of Thomas Cook.

The idea of the tour group, as promoted by Cook, was widely derided right from the beginning. Hostile commentators referred to "Cook's Hordes" and suggested he should dress his flock in uniform. *Punch* magazine went as far as to suggest that Cook's tourists were mental patients

spiky script, complete with ruled footnotes and marginal additions, survives in the Cook company archives. Her identity is a bit of a mystery. She was, though, a resilient character, quite prepared to rough it: her account of a couple of weeks sleeping under canvas in Palestine treats it as a lark, even when torrential rain and wind destroyed several tents on one tempestuous night. She was unperturbed by the reported danger of marauding Bedouin (the party's muleteers carried rifles for protection), and matter-of-fact in mentioning that outside Caesarea they rode past the decomposing body of a "white man," who, they were told, had been killed by Bedouin. She had a sense of fun (she delighted in recording the number of times each member of the party fell off his or her donkey or horse), and she liked shopping.

The only hard information we have about her (her name and sketchy address) comes from a list of all the members of Cook's party that she helpfully includes in her diary:

1. Mr. Dennett	Hotel de Londres, 8 rue St Hyacinthe, Paris
2. Mrs. Dennett	"
3. Henry Newman	Leominster, England
4. Mrs. H. Newman	"
5. Mrs. Rose	Peterbro Villas, Fulham, London, England
6. Miss Crichton	unknown

7. Miss Lines	Shillington, Herts., England	
8. Miss Riggs	Hampstead, London, England	
9. J. Dickson, Esq.	Cleethorpes, Grimsby, England	
10. Mrs. Dickson	"	
11. W.A. Backhouse	Darlington, England	
12. R. Crichton	Skene House, Aberdeen, Scotland	
13. J. Crichton	"	
14. J. Frith, Esq.	Sheffield, England	
15. J. Luckie	Springfield, Haddington, England	
16. A.E. Webb	Bath, England	
17. John Lorn, M.D.	Darlington, England	
18. B.H. Margetts	Huntingdon, England	
19. D. Samuels	16 Warrington Terrace, Maida Vale, London	
20. Mrs. Samuels	"	
21. J.H. MacDonald	Rock Mansion, Brighton	
22. Mrs. MacDonald	"	
23. W. Brewin	Cirencester, England	
24. Mr. D. Witt Hay	Paris	
25. Mrs. Hay	"	
26. G.P. Beeley	Rochdale, England	
27. Miss Porter	Palace Clogher, Northern Ireland	
28. J. Chalmers	37 Albyn Place, Aberdeen, Scotland	
29. J. Cookson	35 Great Avenham Street, Preston, England	
30. Mr. Martin	An American taken on at Alexandria	

Miss Riggs noted in her diary the names and addresses of her twenty-nine fellow travelers in Egypt. She, herself, remains mysterious: the only information we have is that she was a resident of "Hampstead, London, England"

Even as organized by Thomas Cook, the trip to Egypt would not have been cheap: the cost to each person for just the Nile boat portion of the trip was £40, which adjusted to today's prices would be around £3,200, or over $5,000. Mr. and Mrs. Dennett, the Newmans, Mrs. Rose, and their traveling companions had to have been relatively wealthy—or companions or servants of the wealthy—likely well-educated, upper-middle-class people of some standing, used to being waited on and obeyed. (A possible clue to Miss Riggs's identity comes from Thomas Cook's own notes on the Palestine portion of the trip, which mention seven ladies traveling with their husbands, none of which could be "Miss" Riggs; one lady in the company of her parents, who, as there are no other Riggses on the list, is not our diarist; and one "attendant upon a lady of the party"—was Miss Riggs a lady's maid?)

While the group had been in Alexandria, Thomas Cook had gone on ahead to Cairo to negotiate the leasing of some river transport. From the state-owned Azizieh Company, he had managed to secure the use of the *Benha* and the *Beniswaif*—both boats the personal property of Khedive Ismail, as it seemed to Cook was most of everything in the country. The steamers, both British built, were already in semi-regular passenger service on the Nile, departing Cairo once a month from November to February, but they were not generally used by travelers because the departures were unreliable and the boats' schedules didn't make allowances for sightseeing stops.

EGYPT,
AND ARABIA PETRÆA

MOSQUE OF SULTAN HASSAN
GRAND CAIRO

ALEXANDRIA

As master of his own vessels, the always meticulous Thomas Cook set his own schedule, which Miss Riggs dutifully copied into her diary:

Beniswaif [Beni Suef]	2 hours
Minizeh [Minya]	2 hours
Beni Hasan	3 hours
Assiout [Asyut]	5 hours
Girgeh [Girga]	2 hours
Kenah [Qena]	8 hours
Looksor [Luxor]	3 days
Eshneh [Esna]	3 hours
Edfou [Edfu]	6 hours
Koom Ambou [Kom Ombo]	2 hours
Assouan [Aswan]	2 days

OPPOSITE Cook's party planned to sail from Cairo the 740 kilometers (460 miles) to Luxor, where, after a halt of three days, they would continue on another 217 kilometers (135 miles) to Aswan. It was planned the journey upriver would take thirteen days, followed by two days at Aswan and then a straight sail of six days back down to Cairo

Cook did his homework well and, give or take a few tweaks, this is the itinerary most Nile cruises would stick to until security issues halted sailings between Cairo and Luxor in the 1980s.

The party boarded the two boats, sixteen to each, accommodated mostly in two-berth cabins. Miss Riggs's passenger list only includes thirty names, but she mentions elsewhere in her diary that Mr. Martin was accompanied by his brother; the thirty-second person was Thomas Cook himself.

The *Benha* and *Beniswaif* left Cairo late in the afternoon of Wednesday 10 February. Miss Riggs shared a cabin with Miss Porter. Their beds were about half a meter wide, in other words, just sufficient for a person of slim build as long as they weren't too restless, with about the same space for dressing. The ladies were on the *Benha*, which turned out to be the better of the two boats; the *Beniswaif* wasn't as well maintained—a pipe burst, rendering one cabin unusable, and its occupant had to sleep out on deck. As well as being slightly shabby it was troubled by what Cook called "F. sharps," a Victorian euphemism for fleas (bugs were "B. flats"). Miss Riggs's boat also had the better steward, cook, and waiters, and there was some resentment on the *Beniswaif* that Cook chose to travel exclusively on the *Benha*. However, while at Qena, it was the *Benha*'s paddlewheel that broke, causing a day's delay in sailing while it was repaired.

Miss Riggs found the *Benha* acceptable with its daily routine of coffee at eight, breakfast at ten, lunch at one, and dinner at six-thirty. The passengers sat on deck after the evening meal until the sun went down and they were forced inside by the night chill.

The boats would moor at the bank each night, setting off again at 6 a.m., with a great din for at least an hour beforehand as the boilers were brought up to steam. At each stop, Cook would arrange for donkeys to transport his

Summing up the travelers' experience in his time, the French voyager Jean-Jacques Ampère (1800–64) once said that a visit to Egypt was "a donkey ride and a boating trip interspersed with ruins."

charges to whatever sights he'd set upon them seeing. This is where Miss Riggs tended to have issues. At Beni Hasan, the saddles were put on improperly (she had brought her own, a ladies' saddle, all the way from England), so she got off her mount and walked; and then at Karnak the *Benha* party arrived behind the other boat and found all the donkeys already taken.

The Nile was particularly low this year—the locals complained it was the lowest it had been for years—and so hardly a day passed when one of the steamers, or both, did not run aground on sandbanks and had to be hauled by the crew back into deeper waters. This was a source of frequent irritation and, at one point, the passengers on the *Benha* threatened to get off and make their way overland because the crew were sitting around smoking waterpipes rather than engaging in any attempt to refloat the boat.

Other incidents that might have ruffled a Victorian lady's composure are noted in Miss Riggs's diary with what seems like no more than a slightly cocked eyebrow: for instance, when the boat passed the Monastery of Our Lady the Virgin at Sohag and the monks swam from the shore and climbed up on deck, completely naked, asking for baksheesh. (They would pop the coins into their mouths for the swim back.) On future cruises Cook advised ladies to remain in the boat's salon when it was passing the monastery.

Cook's major concern was for the health of his charges. He took onboard at Cairo a ship's doctor. He worried about the effects of the heat on the European disposition and that the sudden temperature drops at night might bring on the chills. He was right to worry: Mrs. Samuels came down sick toward the end of the stay in Egypt and died soon after in Palestine. Cook narrowly escaped death himself, although under very different circumstances. Bathing in the shallows of the river at Luxor he was swept up by a fast-flowing undercurrent and almost drowned. He was saved by boatmen who rowed out and extended an oar for him to grab onto.

It happened that Cook's was not the only English party on the Nile at this time. Albert, the playboy Prince of Wales, eldest son of Queen Victoria and heir apparent to the British throne, had set off from Cairo just four days earlier.★ The royal party sailed in a fleet of five blue and gold steamers, plus a tender, and a towed *dahabiya* (sailboat) that served as the royal couple's

---

★ Albert had also voyaged up the Nile in February 1862, dispatched on a Near East tour by his mother, Queen Victoria, to keep him out of trouble after he had been discovered to be having an affair with a prostitute. This 1869 trip was a sort of second honeymoon with his wife Alexandra but, once again, there was an element of expediency in keeping the future king far away from England because now his name was being linked to a high-profile adultery scandal.

private sleeping quarters. All were provided by the Khedive of Egypt. Each steamer was decorated with scenes depicting incidents from the life of Antony and Cleopatra, and each towed a barge of 'necessities and luxuries,' which between them included three thousand bottles of champagne and four thousand of claret, not to mention sherry, ale, and liqueurs of all sorts. They had horses, a white donkey, and four French chefs, plus a 'stuffer' to deal with all the animals the Prince was going to shoot. (The stuffer, or taxidermist, was renowned Nile explorer and big-game hunter Samuel Baker, later Sir Samuel Baker, governor-general of Sudan.) Although they drank champagne at Karnak beneath a firework display, the temples were otherwise largely ignored by the Prince, who preferred blasting away at anything that flew or stood on four legs. In one day alone he shot twenty-eight flamingoes, keeping Baker, who had his own workshop on deck, busily employed.

The party also gathered other mementos along the way, including a large sarcophagus, thirty mummies, a live black ram, and a ten-year-old Nubian boy, who was taken back to the royal country retreat of Sandringham in England.

The coincidence of the two Nile cruises became a source of excitement on one side, and well-documented irritation on the other. Traveling as part of the Prince's retinue was William Howard Russell, a war correspondent of some renown attached to the London *Times*. He afterward reported that Cook's party had been in "full cry up the river after the Prince and Princess."

Albert, Prince of Wales, and his wife were also on the Nile in early 1869, being transported up river in a lavish royal barge, called the *Alexandra*, towed by a steamer, all provided by the Khedive of Egypt

PREVIOUS SPREAD The Prince of Wales, seated on the rock in the right foreground, and his touring party among the ruins at Karnak; this photograph was taken on the earlier royal visit to Egypt, in 1862

Two of the Prince of Wales's entourage on the Nile. The illustration comes from *A Diary in the East*, by William Howard Russell, the newspaper correspondent who traveled with the royal party

Which was a little harsh, given that he had also written that some of the royal hangers-on themselves were more interested in observing those aboard the royal yacht than in admiring the sites along the Nile. "The proper study of mankind is man," wrote Russell, "particularly if you have good lorgnettes and telescopes." Nevertheless, he was scathing about Cook's clients, who he considered had been inappropriately "thrown off their balances by the prospect of running the Prince and Princess of Wales to earth in a Pyramid, of driving them to bay in the Desert, of hunting them into the recesses of a ruin."

Russell's report of the royal procession frequently references the "pursuit." On Thursday 11 February he records that the royal fleet started off at four o'clock in the morning because it was "fraught with danger of being overtaken by the Tourists." And two mornings later: "The fleet moved off at 5.30 a.m. and went at a steady pace up the river. A steamer was discerned following us far off. 'The tourists are coming!' was the universal cry. Every glass was directed to the ship. At last she was pronounced to be a trading steamer from Cairo, and a feeling of relief was at once experienced."

The royal lead had been cut from four to two days by the time the *Benha* and *Beniswaif* reached Asyut, where Miss Riggs paid a visit to an American Mission School that had just received the Princess. At Luxor, the Cook party was disappointed to find they had arrived just too late, the royals having departed a few hours earlier. They visited the house of the British consul (who was also the U.S. consul) Mustafa Agha, who, according to Russell, was "next to the ruins perhaps the best known 'object' in Thebes." He had entertained the royals at his house, which was within the ruins of Luxor Temple, and Miss Riggs copied the signatures of the Prince and Princess and their companions into her diary.

Cook's steamers did finally catch up with the royal fleet at Aswan (where Miss Riggs bought a scarf with a red border for her hat) but the ships were deserted: the royals had gone to visit Philae, farther upriver. Russell, however, had stayed behind: "Cook's tourists have also arrived!" he wrote. "Their steamers are just below us in the stream. The tourists are all over the place. Some are bathing off the banks; others, with eccentric head-dresses, are toiling through the deep sand. They are just beaten by a head in the race! Another day, and the Prince and Princess would have been at their mercy."★

★ The real issue here was, of course, not concern for the privacy of the Prince and Princess, but pure snobbery. Russell could not bear the thought that the Nile had to be shared with fellow countrymen (and women) of a lower status. "It is a nuisance to the ordinary traveller to have his peace broken," he wrote, although by "ordinary" he clearly meant aristocratic, "to have a flood of people poured into a quiet town,

The salon on the royal barge *Alexandra*. Note the piano: on occasional evenings the royal party would gather here and sing to the accompaniment of piano and bagpipes, possibly much to the bemusement of villages within earshot

Of course, Cook's party pushed on to Philae, only to find that the royals had transferred to *dahabiya*s and sailed on into Nubia, and so out of reach of the tourists, who were going no farther south than Aswan.

Unaware of how he and his group were viewed from the boats ahead, Thomas Cook penned a letter from the *Benha* to the editor of his hometown newspaper, *The Leicester Journal*, in which he regretted that his boats had not managed to catch up with the Prince. "It would have been a real pleasure to have fallen in with this Royal tourist party, with the son of our enthusiastic tourist Queen at its head," he wrote. Later, when Russell published his side of the tale, Cook was greatly offended, and vented his annoyance in letters addressed personally to the Prince of Wales.

For the moment, Cook had little time to reflect. Once back in Cairo, there were a couple more days for sightseeing before the return train journey to Alexandria. Here, the party split and goodbyes were said: some were to take a ship and return directly to Europe, while others, including Miss Riggs, were to be joined by fresh arrivals with whom they would form a new party and sail for Jaffa and on to Beirut to begin a five-week tour of Palestine. With twenty-four travelers, a retinue of thirty-

to have hotels and steamers crammed, to see his pet mountain peak crested with bonnets and wideawakes, to behold his favourite valley filled up with a flood of mere English,"—and here's the awful giveaway—"whom no one knows." Cook aimed to democratize Nile tourism and in years to come, among a certain class of people, he would be despised for it.

Early travelers in Egypt found travel by donkey amusing, if uncomfortable and a little undignified, but mounting a camel was just outright dangerous

three servants, and seventy mules and horses, Cook's caravan made its way from Beirut down the coast via Sidon, Tyre, Haifa, Caesarea, and Ramleh to Jerusalem. There were long days of riding and some foul weather but Cook did what he could to make proceedings as comfortable as possible. "Arrived at Sidon by six," wrote Miss Riggs on 11 March, the first day out of Beirut, "the muleteers had passed us at lunch and our tents were pitched, all very exciting to see our arrangements for the coming month and quite astonished and delighted to see nice little iron bedsteads all put up with mattresses, bolster and Arab blankets striped with red . . . table in the centre and wash basin . . . very smart. Old carpets or rugs laid at each bed: we thought ourselves in clover."

Unfortunately, at about this point Miss Riggs fills all the available pages in her diary, well before her adventure is over. We know from Thomas Cook's own account that the party went on to Damascus and then returned via Beirut to Constantinople, Trieste, Venice, Milan, Como, Zurich, and Paris, before finally arriving back in England 105 days after departing London Bridge. Perhaps there was a second diary but, if so, it has not survived. Instead, we have to leave her on 25 March, determinedly exploring Jerusalem: "outside the walls to Zion Gate to David's and Solomon's tomb; so windy we could hardly stand . . . back through the leper quarter—a fearful sight. Stopped at the bazaars . . . took the Via Dolorosa, which leads in direct line to St. Stephens Gate. Passed other entrances to the Mosk of Omar, the Moslems."

Although she never says so herself, reading between the lines I think it is reasonable to suggest that Miss Riggs found her expedition to Egypt and Palestine never less than fascinating.

As for Cook himself, he was in no doubt as to the success of the venture, and particularly the Egypt portion of the expedition. A few days after leaving Alexandria, at a desk in Beirut, he put pen to paper to sum up his thoughts: "My tour to the Nile was a great event in the arrangements of modern travel," he wrote.

He was more right than he could know: Thomas Cook's arrival in Egypt would not only change the nature of travel there, but in some ways it would change the country itself.

FOUR MONTHS IN A DAHABIYA

"There is no hotel in Europe, from Morley's or the Hôtel du Louvre down to the vile inn at Capua, in which the traveler will live so well in all respects as on his Nile boat." WILLIAM COWPER PRIME, 1874

Intrepid as Miss Riggs's journey seems today, the route she followed was, even at the time, already well worn.

When Napoleon Bonaparte invaded Egypt on 1 July 1798, done in order to undermine Britain's access to India, it was the beginning of an inglorious three years, during which time his army was ravaged by plague and his fleet sunk. But while a failure in military terms, the brief French occupation had a lasting impact on Egypt and its place in the world in other ways. In addition to 54,000 soldiers and 400 ships, Napoleon brought along a second army, this one composed of 160 scientists, engineers, scholars, and artists. Their job was to capture not Egyptian territory, but its geography, topography, zoology, flora, culture, society, and history. They measured, mapped, and drew their way from north to south, recording everything they encountered. After their return to France in 1801, the work continued and, in 1809, the first volumes of the *Description de l'Égypte* were published (there would eventually be twenty-three; thirty-seven in the second edition). There had been other, earlier works on the country, but with its 894 plates, comprising over 3,000 drawings, and including a volume of maps, there had never been anything quite like this before. The sheer physical size of the work, the low number of copies made, and its high price, limited its accessibility to only the elite of society, but it was enough.

The *Description* catalogued an almost unimaginable array of wonders, but perhaps the most significant single item it showed was a large inscribed stela that had been discovered in July 1799 by French soldiers strengthening coastal defenses at Rosetta. Though ceded to the British under the terms by which the French extricated themselves from Egypt, copies of the stone's trilingual inscriptions were made and, from these, in 1822, the Frenchman Jean-François Champollion was able to crack the code of hieroglyphics.

It was now possible to begin to understand the language and mind of the ancient Egyptians, a development that gave birth to the science of modern Egyptology, and launched a fleet of scholars and adventurers bound

Before the coming of the packaged tourist a journey up the Nile was the province of the gentlemanly adventurer, explorer, and amateur scholar

for Egypt. At the same time, the power vacuum that had been left by the withdrawal of the French army from Egypt had been filled by a former Macedonian mercenary by the name of Muhammad Ali, who, after years of civil war, pacified the country. Unlike his predecessors, the new pasha was eager for western knowledge to help develop his new domain, and he welcomed foreign visitors and diplomatic representations.

Perhaps 'science' isn't quite the right word to apply to Egyptology at this point, because for many of its earliest practitioners it was more of a treasure hunt. Men like the French consul-general Bernardino Drovetti and the British consul-general Henry Salt via his agent, the former circus strongman Giovanni Belzoni, were engaged in a competition to amass the greatest collection of Egyptian antiquities they could in order to sell them to museums back in Europe and America. Even the scholarly Jean-François Champollion wasn't immune from such rapaciousness, removing a wall panel from the tomb of Seti in the Valley of the Kings in 1828.

But there were others who came simply to observe and record, such as John Gardner Wilkinson, who arrived in 1821 and later became famed for his *The Manners and Customs of the Ancient Egyptians* (1837); Edward William Lane, who disembarked in Alexandria in 1825 to collect information for his *Manners and Customs of the Modern Egyptians* (1836); artist Robert Hay, who was in Egypt from 1824 until 1828, and 1829 to 1834, recording monuments and inscriptions; and the prolific David Roberts, whose two years in Egypt and Palestine (1838–40) provided him with raw material for a further ten years of work producing the superbly detailed plates that made up his *Sketches in the Holy Land* and *Syria and Egypt & Nubia* folios.

The books and the prints were hungrily received by a public excited by the little-known world they portrayed. As novelist William Thackeray, author of *Vanity Fair*, and a visitor to Egypt in 1844, noted, "There is a fortune to be made for painters in Cairo … and should any artist read this, who has leisure, and wants to break new ground, let him take heart, and try a winter in Cairo, where there is the finest climate and the best subjects for his pencil." Tellingly, Thackeray's trip was paid for by the Peninsular and Oriental Steam Navigation Company, later P&O, which had just won a contract to deliver mail to Alexandria, and was keen to promote its new steamer route to Egypt. Not only was the world becoming ever more fascinated by the land of the Nile, but the land of the Nile was also becoming increasingly accessible.

The first proper English-language guidebook to the country, Murray's *Handbook for Travellers in Egypt* (1847), was prepared by John Gardner Wilkinson, and was a condensed and updated version of a more academic previous work, *Modern Egypt and Thebes*. With it, we enter into the era of the scholarly amateur traveler. Although increasingly accessible, it was still a very select group who could afford the time and money to travel to Egypt. But there were plenty who qualified, and from the mid-nineteenth century Egypt became an optional extension of the European Grand Tour. A great

The nineteenth-century vogue for the mysterious and alluring "Orient" drew large numbers of painters to Egypt and the Middle East, including the German Gustav Bauernfeind, who, unusually, included himself in "A Street Scene in Damascus" (1887)

Der Kadige.
noon — 1. P.M.
Jan. 2. 1867
(28)

many of those who visited tidied up their journal notes, letters, and sketches and had them published, inspiring in turn the next wave of travelers.

The earliest travelers from Europe and America came to Egypt by sea, usually via Malta. Once at Alexandria, visitors usually hastened on to Cairo by taking a boat up the Rosetta branch of the Nile (or after 1856, the train). Cairo could occupy anything from a few days to a month or two, then inevitably one would set off up the Nile, for, as American artist Charles Dana Gibson wrote, "To go to Egypt and not go up the Nile is like standing outside a theater watching the audience go in, and then waiting until they come out, to glean from their conversation some idea of the play."

Travel in Egypt has almost always involved the Nile, both the nation's life-giving artery and its main highway. The ancient Egyptians attached such importance to the river that their mythology had Ra, the sun god, travel across the sky every day in a boat. They used boats themselves to travel, fish, hunt, trade, make war, and in ceremonies of worship. Their kings and pharaohs were buried with boats of one kind or another: there is the solar boat discovered in a pit at Giza, the full-sized vessel buried around 2500 BC, intended for use in the afterlife by the king Khufu (Cheops), in whose honor the Great Pyramid was built; thirty-five wooden models of various boats were discovered in the tomb of King Tutankhamun.

In his *Handbook for Travellers*, Gardner Wilkinson described some of the numerous boat types that were in use on the Nile: the *djerm* was the largest and only used on the river during the annual inundation;★ the *gyasa* was a freight boat, as was the *aggub*, which was unique in having a square sail (all the rest have triangular sails); the *garib* was a fishing boat, the *maadéëh* a ferry. There were also three types of vessel, he noted, that were well adapted for traveling on the river, being furnished with cabins: there was the large *maash*, also known as a *ráhleh*, a basic vessel found in rural regions, but better suited for the traveler were the *dahabiya* (which Gardner Wilkinson spells *dahabéëh*) and the smaller *cangia*.

The latter two, which were the rough equivalents of the European yacht, were the boats of choice for travelers, particularly the larger *dahabiya*. This

A beautiful pea-green boat...
Best known as the author of nonsense verse, like *The Owl and the Pussycat*, the short-sighted and sickly Edward Lear was a committed artist-traveler who visited Egypt no less than four times between 1849 and 1872. He undertook two journeys up the Nile, in 1853–54 and 1866–67, sketching prolifically on both occasions. These pencils and watercolor washes were later worked up into some forty large oil paintings of topography and ancient monuments. Perhaps uniquely, Lear was also captivated by the boats he passed on the Nile and he made a great number of studies of them (*opposite*). As he explained in a letter home, "The most beautiful feature is the number of boats, which look like giant moths, —& sometimes there is a fleet of 20 or 30 in sight at once."

★ The annual rainy season on the uppermost central east African reaches of the Nile caused a rising of the waters each June. This would continue until it reached a peak in September, after which the water would gradually subside until the following June, when the cycles began again. In Upper Egypt, the rise could be as much as thirty feet. The river in flood was far easier to navigate. The annual floods were dramatically lessened with the completion of the first Aswan Dam in 1902, and completely halted by the construction of the High Dam in the 1960s.

A Mamluk-era royal barge, or *dahabiya*, illustrated in Georg Ebers' *Egypt: Historical, Descriptive, and Picturesque*. It is possible these craft were inspired by the royal barges of Venice, which was an important trading partner with Egypt in medieval times

was a style of boat that had its origins in the ceremonial barges used by the Mamluk sultans from the thirteenth century onward to celebrate the opening of the Grand Canal of Cairo, which happened each year at the start of the annual Nile flood. The name means 'the golden one' (from the Arabic for gold, *dahab*), which suggests these imperial vessels would have been wonderfully ornate and gilded. The original 'golden ships' were huge affairs with sixty oars; however, by the nineteenth century the river boats whose design they inspired were much more modest, mostly between forty and one hundred feet in length. They were shallow and flat-bottomed, with masts supporting two large sails capable of capturing the lightest of breezes. There was a cabin at the stern, occupying a quarter to a third of the length of the deck, and its roof served as a raised, open-air salon covered by an awning. The crew kept to the deck, sleeping in the open at night, and there was a small shed-like affair right up near the prow, as far from the cabin as possible, which was the kitchen.

The first task for the would-be Nile traveler was selecting a boat. This could be far from straightforward. While in 1845, traveler Isabella Romer could congratulate herself on securing the only three decent *dahabiya*s on the river, twenty-eight years later when Amelia Edwards visited the moorings at Bulaq, Cairo's river port, she was confronted with two or three hundred boats for hire. "Now, most persons know something of the miseries of house-hunting," she wrote in *A Thousand Miles up the Nile*, "but only those who have experienced them know how much keener are the miseries of *dahabiya* hunting."

The boats for hire were all much the same with just slight variations in configuration and cleanliness, not to mention cost, with prices rising according to the size of boat and number of crew. Just as important as finding the right boat was being satisfied that it was helmed by a trustworthy *rais*, or captain. Every *rais* eagerly presented the certificates given to him by former travelers, although, as Edwards noted, the same certificates mysteriously turned up again and again on board different boats, and in the hands of different captains. For ten days, Edwards put in three or four hours every morning in her search for the perfect boat, a task not helped by the fact that they were given to changing moorings. Hire rates also fluctuated according to the number of westerners looking for boats on any given day. Edwards found the whole experience with its deliberating, haggling, and hesitating to be "miserable."

In addition to the captain, the standard staffing on a *dahabiya* ran to six to eight sailors, a steersman, and a kitchen boy, all of whose wages had to be agreed on. Once all this had been settled, a contract had to be written up and signed by both parties; this was usually done at a consulate in the presence of an Arabic translator. Gardner Wilkinson advised that travelers should make it clear to the *rais* that he is not to take any other passengers or merchandise of any kind, that the whole boat shall be at the traveler's command, and that no one was to quit the boat on the pretext of visiting relatives without asking permission.

Boats moored at the port of Bulaq in Cairo. By the 1870s prospective Nile voyagers could find between two and three hundred vessels here for hire

He also recommended that the first thing to be done after hiring a boat was to have it sunk to rid it of rats and other vermin, and then refloated and thoroughly cleaned. Traveling alone, British artist William Henry Bartlett hired a thirty-foot, twin-masted *cangia* at Bulaq in the summer of 1845. He grumbled at the prices—"the price of every thing in Egypt seems to have greatly risen of late years, the hire of boats in particular"—but more so at the bugs onboard that caused his first night to be sleepless and savage: "The scoundrel of a *rais* had neglected to sink the boat as he had promised, and from every chink and crevice in the old planks hundreds came forth, scenting the blood of an Englishman." He had the crew throw all the mats overboard and scrub every inch of the boat, stuffing any chinks and cracks with camphor. However, they couldn't get rid of the rats infesting the storeroom and Bartlett had to resign himself to living with them.

Ms. M.L.M. Carey and party, traveling up the Nile in the winter of 1860–61, fifteen years after Bartlett, did not have their boat sunk before sailing because they were told it was unnecessary. They later came to regret this when they discovered their clothes and other possessions gnawed away. They took two cats onboard as a counter-measure.

Very quickly, as *dahabiya*s became larger, more elaborate, and better maintained, the practice of preventive sinking stopped. Amelia Edwards in 1873 makes no mention of it.

Ms. Carey recorded her travails in one of the more readable and entertaining Nile travelogues, *Four Months in a Dahabëëh*. As Miss Riggs would do eight and a half years later, the Carey party set off from London Bridge station, only they were traveling independently and headed to Marseilles from where they sailed on the P&O steamer *Vectis*. One of their fellow passengers was Ferdinand de Lesseps, who the previous year had broken ground on his Suez Canal project.

On reaching Cairo, they had rooms reserved at Shepheard's, which they found full with other parties from their own steamer and another just

The layout of a typical, medium-sized *dahabiya* squeezed in berths for four passengers, with a salon for dining and a quarterdeck above the cabin for daytime use. The crew slept on deck

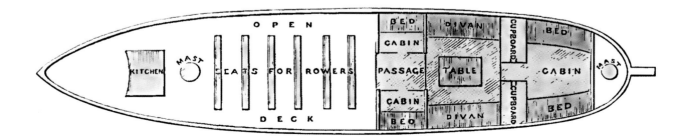

Travelers arrive at Bulaq, where their luggage is portered aboard the boat that will be their home for the next three or four months

in from Southampton. The search for a *dahabiya* took three visits but was resolved in a relatively simple way because only one boat was found that offered the party's required accommodation of five separate cabins.

So far, Ms. Carey had been traveling light: a few common dresses for the river; a shawl for the daytime and warm wraps for the night; round hats, neckerchiefs, veils, gauntleted gloves, and large, lined umbrellas; two pairs of strong boots; galoshes for the mud on the banks of the Nile; elderflower water for the eyes and the complexion; a preparation of zinc as a cure for ophthalmia; and, for reference, Murray's *Handbook for Travellers*, Gardner Wilkinson's *The Manners and Customs of the Ancient Egyptians*, and Eliot Warburton's 1845 Middle Eastern travelogue *The Crescent and the Cross*. Supplies now had to be laid in for the Nile voyage, and these were purchased at Turnbull's shop in the Frank Street, where they were shown samples of biscuits, rice, pickles, lemonade syrup, tea, sugar, and jam. The negotiating of the purchases was left to the dragoman, the all-purpose guide, valet, translator, and traveling companion every party of travelers hired to help them navigate the unfamiliarities of Egypt.

In their rooms at the hotel the crates and boxes containing everything necessary for furnishing and provisioning a floating home piled up, from linen, teapots, and feather brushes, to foot baths, insect powder, and lanterns. This was in no way extravagant: other travelers, including Amelia Edwards, took a piano or a complete library. It was a tradition that every *dahabiya* flew the national flag of the party aboard, as well as a distinguishing flag of its own, so friends could recognize one another on the river. Ms. Carey's party chose a crocodile for its symbol, and had one put onto a flag, and also purchased a couple of Union Jacks. (The cloth merchants of the bazaar must have been doing good business out of all this flag provisioning.) Muhammad, the dragoman, also provided a hammer and chisel so the party could inscribe their names in rock at certain points in the voyage.★

The Carey party settled aboard their boat, which was named the *Cairo*, on the evening of Thursday 15 November 1860. There had been a hope they might leave the moorings that night for somewhere quieter—a dervish festival was being celebrated at a mosque immediately facing the *Cairo*—but the boat wasn't ready and so Ms. Carey and a companion settled for joining the crowds on the quayside and pushing their way through to where a circle of small lamps on poles illuminated a circle of "rocking, dancing, and screaming" worshipers, a spectacle they found disturbing, and which sent them back to the refuge of their new floating home.

This was a *dahabiya* of ninety-seven feet in length and fourteen feet two inches in width. There were four cabins, each of roughly six feet by four-and-a-half feet, with sliding doors that let onto a central passage, and a stern cabin of twelve feet in length, the extra space being used for storage of trunks and such. Additionally, there were drawers or cupboards for clothes under every bed. There was also a saloon with a table big enough for six at dinner, two mirrors, and bookshelves. Over all this was the quarterdeck, with divans on either side, a table, a chair or two, and an awning. The crew lived on the lower deck, and slept out in the open air. In the bow was a kitchen. The larger of the two masts was fixed toward the bow, the smaller one in the stern. Twelve oars were provided for rowing, and a number of long poles for pushing off from sandbanks. Altogether there were an astonishing twenty-three people on board: five passengers, the dragoman, *rais*, steersman, fourteen crewmen, and a cook.

They weren't able to set sail on the Friday either, because the winds were against them. The Nile flows from south to north, but the prevailing wind blows from north to south, enabling the boats to sail against the current.

★ American journalist William Cowper Prime, who traveled in Egypt in 1855–56, offered the following advice on dealing with dragomans: "The dragoman may be defined as the gentleman who travels with you," he wrote. "He becomes a part of yourself, goes where you go, sleeps where you sleep, you talk through him, buy through him (and pay him and through him at the same time), and, in point of fact, you become his servant. But, if you choose otherwise, you may make him what he should be, a very good servant, and nothing more. He who can not manage his own servants should stay at home and not travel."

As most *dahabiya*s looked alike, travelers flew a flag indicating their nationality, as well as a flag with a personal motif so they could be identified by friends and acquaintances on the Nile

However, winds from the south are not uncommon and, in such conditions, faring upstream against both current and wind is impossible. Eventually, on Saturday, the wind changed and the *Cairo* was able to start on its way upriver.

The minimum time for a trip up the Nile and back was considered to be three months. The best season for setting out was October, when the cool weather begins and northerly winds prevail. At the beginning of October, boats would also gain the benefit of the Nile flood, when the high waters significantly reduced the chance of running aground on sandbanks.

Once underway, the journey up the Nile was usually made as quickly as possible while the winds were favorable. Halts at places of interest were reserved for the journey back, when the *dahabiya* could coast on the current, aided and steered by oars. An extract from the diary of Marianne Brocklehurst, who was on the Nile at the same time as Amelia Edwards, provides an illustration of how the traveler was at the mercy of the winds:

> Saturday, March 7
> [We] make a start at one o'clock, only to stick at the sandbank near the telegraph office at three by reason of contrary winds. Let no one who has not patience come to the Nile!

> Sunday, March 8
> Go about 10 miles. Wind south and strong.

> Monday, March 9
> Stuck fast all day.

Winds could, on occasion, be more than exasperating: they could be lethal. Stretches where the river was hemmed in by cliffs were prone to sudden squalls that could capsize a boat: in January 1876 a *dahabiya* was overturned with the loss of all but one member of crew and one passenger. A few years later the *dahabiya* carrying the editor of the *Daily Telegraph* Edwin Arnold, along with his wife and daughter, was capsized near Asyut with loss of life.

Stops while going upriver were usually restricted to those necessary to take onboard fresh produce bought from villagers: chickens, pigeons, even a sheep, eggs, and milk—although William Henry Bartlett had his own goat aboard to supply milk, and in 1910 the daughter of multimillionaire financier Sir Ernest Cassel took her own cow.

Crews usually made their own bread, baking it in the communal ovens at villages along the river, then laying it out on deck to dry in the sun. It was typically served soaked in a lentil soup for breakfast, lunch, or dinner—sometimes all three.

With the city left behind, days onboard would settle into a languorous routine. Some travelers had problems with the heat, or issues with flies and mosquitoes, or basic and repetitive food, but most found river life beguiling. Despite the bugs and rats, William Henry Bartlett quickly came around to life on the Nile.

Travelers frustrated at being becalmed had the option of instructing the crew to get out and pull

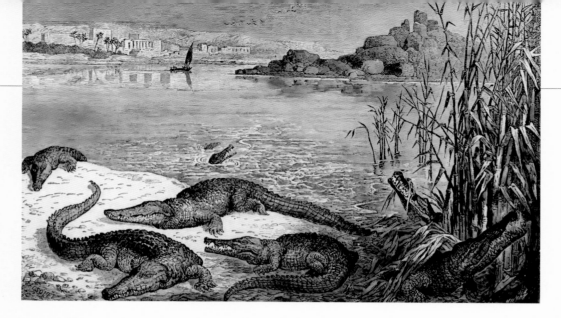

The retreat of the Nile crocodile

"A voyage up the Nile without the sight of a crocodile must appear strangely incomplete, since there is hardly a book of travel that does not abound in feats of marksmanship at the expense of the sacred animal." This was William Henry Bartlett, writing in 1849. He might have had in mind Eliot Warburton, who in *The Crescent and the Cross*, published four years earlier, had excitedly declared, "The first time a man fires at a crocodile is an epoch in his life."

Warburton claimed to have seen hundreds of crocodiles of all sizes as he journeyed up to Wadi Halfa and back, and "fired enough shots at them for a Spanish revolution," but he ruefully admitted to not bagging any. Other travelers were more lethal. The Prince of Wales shot and killed a Nile crocodile in 1869 (a female, nine feet long, found to have eighty eggs inside her), and in 1873 Marianne Brocklehurst passed a *dahabiya* with two strung from its cross pole, while hearing tales of persons unknown who had just shot "four, seven, eleven, any number you like."

The greater threat was from the locals. Crocodiles are opportunistic and indiscriminate predators, and they will lie in wait in shallows and lunge at anything that comes in range, people included. Warburton was told of an old woman who had been gathering water near Qena when she was seized by

a crocodile, which pulled her under and then swam with her to the opposite bank, where the villagers saw the creature feeding on her "as an otter might upon a salmon." But the Egyptians didn't hunt crocodiles for this reason: they hunted them to sell to foreign travelers, many of whom thought a stuffed crocodile made a fine souvenir of Egypt.

As the numbers of tourists increased, crocodiles became scarcer. In 1849, Bartlett reported they could be found as far north as Minya but by the time of Marianne Brocklehurst they were never seen north of Luxor. The increase in the numbers of noisy, wash-creating Nile steamers drove the reptiles still further south, and by the 1880s they were no longer seen north of the First Cataract. Traveling in the winter of 1885–86, in a *dahabiya* appropriately enough called *Timsah* ('crocodile'), the Reverend Archibald Sayce, stopping at Silsila, between Luxor and Aswan, saw what he claimed was one of the last crocodiles left north of the First Cataract: it was dead, recently killed by villagers, who said that when they cut the animal open they found the four hoofs of a donkey and the two earrings of a donkey boy. Sayce adds that by 1890 there were no crocodiles left in the Egyptian Nile; the creation of the Aswan Dam a decade later ensured that this remained the case.

The breezes on the river are so refreshing that I slept far better in my little cabin than at Cairo. I was always up and dressed at a very early hour, often before sunrise; and nothing can be more delicious than these morning experiences on the broad bosom of the river, gliding alongside the shore in the freshness and serenity of dawn. One delight of this mode of travel is that you are always at home with nature; for weeks one never misses seeing the sun rise and set in the same unrivalled splendour. As the wind was often light in the forenoon, it afforded an opportunity for taking a walk, sometimes of some miles, along the raised bank, before the heat grew intense; and this habit was at once healthy, and affords every opportunity of enjoying the rich variety of cultivation which adorns the valley, as well as of gaining an insight into the habits of the population.

Aside from the provisioning stops, there was a variety of rituals that punctuated life under sail. Of these, the most vexing was possibly becoming stuck on a sandbank. The shape of the riverbed changed all the time, and the *rais* had to be on constant watch for the telltale signs of shallow water. Frequently they were not watchful enough.

"Now we are stuck on a mud-bank," recorded Ms. Carey. "The crew start to their feet, seize the boat-poles, and sticking them into the mud, push away with all their strength, bending themselves double as they walk along the side of the boat one after the other, and then withdrawing them, return quickly to repeat the operation. It is of no avail, and three of them proceed to take off their clothes, jump into the water, and put their shoulders to the boat; and while their fellows continue pushing as before from the deck, they lift the huge weight until we float again."

Every now and again, a whole day was put aside for washing linen and clothes. This was carried out by the crew on deck using hot water from a kettle boiled over a fire on the riverbank. Everything was hung to dry off the boat poles, which were stuck in the mud beside the moored *dahabiya*. Ms. Carey's maid, Sarah, was then obliged to spend two days ironing ("The Arabs wash well enough, but the iron is beyond them").

Another marker was the sighting of one's first crocodile. Ms. Carey and party saw theirs stretched on a bank in the middle of the river just upriver of Edfu. They fired off a gun to see if it would move, and watched it scurry into the water. She informed her readers that the Nile between Luxor and Aswan "abounds with crocodiles"—although this would not be the case for too much longer.

PREVIOUS SPREAD Moored *dahabiya*s photographed by Frank Mason Good sometime in the 1860s

A gun was a vital bit of equipment for a voyage up the Nile. Not only was there abundant shooting to be had, but firing off a volley served as the standard greeting when encountering other boats

Reptiles weren't the only exotic beasts encountered. At Aswan, they were taken to view two young lions aboard a cargo boat belonging to a rich merchant, which were being taken down to Cairo for sale. They were offered to Ms. Carey for a gold coin each by their Nubian captor; she sensibly declined. However, Muhammad the dragoman bought a monkey, which he aimed to sell on at Alexandria for a decent profit.

There were no hunters in Ms. Carey's party but the boat carried a gun, as did most all *dahabiya*s, not only for firing off at basking crocodiles, but also to deliver salutes. It was the custom that on arriving at any new place a greeting shot was fired once for every other *dahabiya* that was found lying there; it was expected that those boats would then reply in like manner.

Bang! "Hello there!"

Bang! "Hello there, yourself!"

Even at this time, however (which is still the relatively early year of 1860), the practice was dying out, much to the dismay of the Careys' dragoman Muhammad: "Don't know what's come to English this year. All English, always fired before. But now, none."

The reason was surely the rise in numbers of boats on the Nile, which was steadily increasing year by year. When the *Cairo* arrived at Luxor it

was to find the waterfront obscured by a fleet of eleven other *dahabiya*s, which would have required a barrage of twenty-two shots for all present to exchange their hellos. Later, when the *Cairo* was moored at Wadi Halfa, the report of a gun announced the arrival of a *dahabiya* under the American flag, then again that evening another shot announced the arrival of a third vessel. "Selina and I, though very sociably disposed in general," wrote Ms. Carey, "became alarmed, for we agreed that the charm and romance of sailing on the Nile would be destroyed rather than enhanced by the constant presence of other parties."

William Cowper Prime had expressed similar sentiments at Wadi Halfa five years earlier. "The romance of travel is well-nigh over," he sighed, before opening a bottle of Château Lafitte up on the rocks at Abusir. He then returned to his boat to dine on a turkey "made drunk on brandy," roast goose, roasted teal, curried chicken, pigeon pie, calves'-feet jelly, and a whole lamb stuffed with almonds, raisins, and rice, followed by blancmange, apricot, apple and pumpkin pies, and a cake made of sugar and almonds, from out of which, when it was cut, flew a white pigeon. Well, it was Christmas.

Prime was wrong—well fed, but wrong. The romance of sailing the Nile was far from over. If anything, it was to intensify. *Dahabiya*s became larger in size (the smaller *cangia* had almost completely disappeared from the river by the mid-1860s) and ever more luxurious. Whereas previously cabin space had occupied as little as a quarter of the deck, by the 1880s it was more like three-quarters on some boats, allowing for more and bigger bedrooms and salons. Some hulls were now cast from iron rather than hammered together from wood, making them more robust and longer lasting, although the flip side was that in the case of an accident a wooden hull could be easily patched up locally, whereas iron hulls had to go into dry dock and took an age and considerable expense to repair.

The reason *dahabiya*s became more luxurious was as a reaction to the arrival of the passenger steamer, an innovation that served to polarize Nile travel. As Thomas Cook opened up the Nile to parties of tourists, the *dahabiya* became the preserve of the privileged. Those who could afford to would continue to favor sail over steam, but after 1870 the *dahabiya* was no longer the default means of transportation.

A Monopoly on the Nile

"The Tour up the Nile has become so popular that very soon no American out on a 'European Tour' will dare to return home and face his friends if he has not done the Orient." ROBERT ETZENSBERGER, 1872

Six months after the completion of his successful first organized tour to Egypt and Palestine, Thomas Cook was back. Throughout the summer of 1869, from his offices in London, he had advertised his intention of leading a party to attend the opening ceremonies of the Suez Canal, which were to take place in November. However, this time around he'd struggled to come to agreement with any of the Mediterranean shipping companies and the best he could come up with was ten places on the Austrian Lloyd steamer *America*. On the plus side, those who signed up were not just going to be observers, they would be participants, because the *America* was going to join the inaugural grand steamboat parade that would process through the Canal to the Red Sea.

On Tuesday 9 November, Cook and his small group joined the other sixty or so passengers at Trieste, boarded their ship, and departed Italy. The voyage down the Adriatic was broken by a few hours spent on the island of Corfu, followed by two days of uncomfortably heavy weather, until on the fifth day the ship came in sight of Egypt. That evening she cast anchor with the lights of Port Said in view.

Early the following morning, the *America* approached the harbor and took its position among what Cook estimated to be about seventy steamers, men-of-war, and various other ships of all nations, most fully dressed with national flags. Behind her was the frigate *Greif* carrying the emperor of Austria, whose arrival was met with a volley of cannons. Throughout the rest of that day the firing went on at intervals, as more heads of state and royalty arrived. The greatest barrage was reserved for the arrival of the *Aigle*, which steamed slowly into the harbor on the morning of Tuesday 16 November bearing the guest of honor, the French empress Eugénie.

The man-of-the-hour, Ferdinand de Lesseps, accompanied by Khedive Ismail, and a procession of crowned heads went onboard to pay their respects. In the afternoon religious ceremonies took place; personal guests of the khedive gathered in a grand pavilion, before which were two more

OPPOSITE In the decade 1870–80 Thomas Cook consolidated its presence in Egypt, opening an office at Shepheard's Hotel in Cairo and making sure its boats were the only passenger steamers on the Nile

Among the guests present at the celebrations to mark the inauguration of the Suez Canal were the French empress Eugénie, Austrian emperor Franz Joseph, Norwegian playwright Henrik Ibsen, French painter Jean-Léon Gérôme, German Egyptologist Richard Lepsius, and British tour operator Thomas Cook

pavilions, one for Muslim dignitaries and one for Christian, with stages for the speeches, which went on throughout the afternoon. Thomas Cook managed to place himself at the center of the triangle formed by the three pavilions, from where he had a clear view of all the pageantry. He did not, however, manage to secure an invitation to the grand soirée and ball thrown on the imperial yacht that night and had to content himself with the spectacle of Port Said ablaze with light from the assembled ships, which were hung up to their mastheads with colorful lanterns.

The next morning, at 8:30 a.m., the *Aigle* steamed out of the harbor, followed at intervals of ten to fifteen minutes by forty more vessels; the *America* was the thirty-sixth ship in the procession, and it was not until two in the afternoon that she passed the columns at the entrance to the canal. That night was spent moored a few miles short of Lake Timsah, where the front runners in the procession had dropped anchor. The sail continued the next day, with *America* reaching the festively bedecked town of Ismailiya, where its passengers were entertained in large temporary saloons in which thousands dined and drank champagne and wine at the expense of the khedive; there were military displays and dancing, with fireworks closing the night. Rather than return to their boats, guests could sleep ashore in tents specially provided for the occasion, which were kitted out with beds and bedding.

On Friday 19 November, the *Aigle* again sailed off at the head of the procession, but an overly large French-flagged steamer ran aground where the canal exited the lake and at least half the boats were stuck behind it unmoving for the remainder of the day. It wasn't until Saturday afternoon that the *America* could get underway again; it caught up with the flotilla and halted for the night just outside Suez, finally entering the Red Sea at lunchtime the next day. By Sunday afternoon over forty ships had made the voyage from sea to sea, and the canal was officially opened.

Cook described his passage through the Suez Canal as "one of the red-letter days of my tourist life." Not to mention, of course, that the new waterway also served to open up new opportunities for his rapidly growing business. When, a little under three years later, Cook took off on his first round-the-world tour, taking a party via America to Japan, China, Ceylon, and India, and back via Egypt, the wonder was that he hadn't done it sooner. (The advance announcements for Cook's global odyssey may have been the inspiration for Jules Verne's *Around the World in Eighty Days*, first published that same year, 1872.)

While Thomas was globetrotting, the job of keeping the ship steady at home fell to his only son. Born in 1834, John Mason Cook (Mason was his mother's maiden name) was inducted into the family business at an early age: as a seven-year-old boy he had been onboard that very first Thomas Cook excursion from Leicester to Loughborough. His career as a personal guide began at age ten when he helped escort five hundred other small children on a picnic by rail from Leicester. As a child he became an expert on train timetables, and developed a love of facts and detail—in later life he became a fan of the Sherlock Holmes stories and, on one occasion, reputedly tracked down a thief himself and recovered the stolen goods. Aged fourteen, he personally conducted a party of tourists from London to Scotland, and the following year led groups to Wales and Ireland. After a spell pursuing his

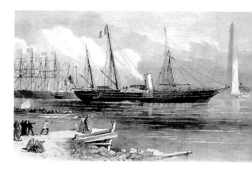

The French steamship the *Aigle* carried Empress Eugénie and led the procession into the Suez Canal

Some forty ships made their way, nose-to-tail, through the Suez Canal; Thomas Cook and his party aboard the *America* were thirty-sixth in the procession

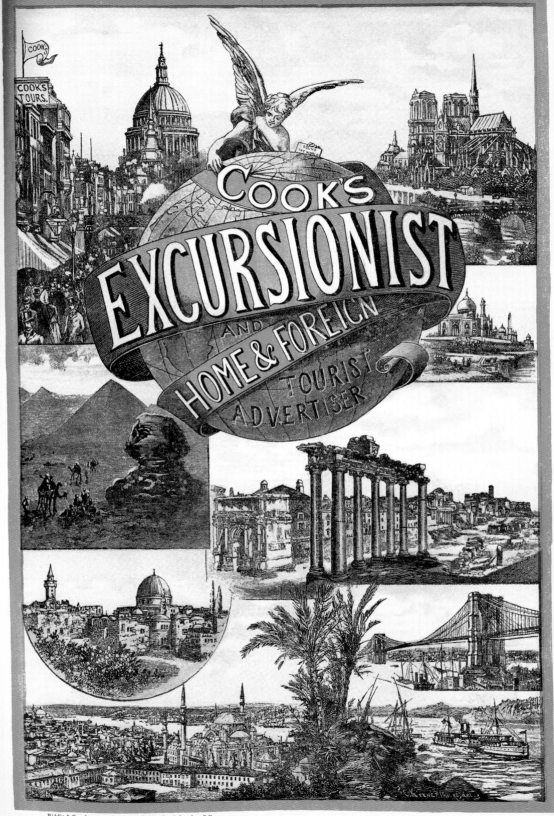

independence, during which time he worked for the Midland Railway and as a self-employed printer, John reunited with his father. He was put in charge of the company's London office, which had the effect of liberating Thomas from his desk and enabling him to pursue new schemes and adventures.

Thomas had led the company's first two Egypt tours but John chaperoned the next, in January 1870. In addition to those who traveled with him from Britain, John managed to sign up additional passengers in Cairo, necessitating a request to the Egyptian government for a bigger boat. He was given the steamer *Beherah*, which had only ever previously been used by guests of the khedive, but was the only boat able to accommodate all of Cook's forty-four passengers. John then personally conducted upriver the largest party of tourists to date on the Nile. Back in Cairo they were met by Thomas at the head of a second party, and the whole lot were led off to Palestine, followed by Constantinople and Athens.

Despite the expense—for the hire of the *Beherah* Cook had to pay the astronomical sum of £1,848 in gold—it was clear to John, who was a shrewder businessman than his father, that there was great opportunity in Egypt. The business of Thomas Cook was seasonal, operating primarily between Easter and early fall, when the climate in Europe and America was generally warm and travel was unlikely to be hindered by bad weather. By contrast, Egypt was far too hot for westerners to endure during the summer months and was best suited to visiting in winter. Adding Egypt and Palestine to Cook's annual program would mean that the company could pursue year-round business. Thomas might initially have been led to the Holy Land by piety, but in John's mind it was profit that would keep the Cooks coming back.

He was in Egypt again that November, this time accompanying a family party upriver on a *dahabiya*, which he had organized for them. While there, he met with the khedive's administration and negotiated the rights for the firm of Thomas Cook to be the sole agency for the Nile steamer passenger service.

The expansion in Egypt coincided with a major development in the Thomas Cook company. In 1871, John became an equal partner with his father in the family firm, which from that time on was Thomas Cook & Son. It was a strained partnership, as the pair held wildly differing views on how the business should be run, but in the first months of that year the newly branded Cook & Son organized several tours of varying lengths from London to Egypt and Palestine, including a 106-day tour that took in a trip up the Nile; an eighty-six-day trip that was Cairo and Palestine only; and

All the world in print
To help advertise his tours and fares, Thomas Cook created a magazine for his clients. *Cook's Excursionist* is an early forerunner of the modern travel magazine, with its articles on what to see (the 1 April 1868 issue describes where in Paris visitors can view the guillotine), letters from readers, and well-targeted advertising. Even in the 1880s the link to Thomas's origins is still there in the many notices for temperance hotels. Elsewhere, travelers are invited to consider Cox's Pedometer, "for registering the distance traversed by pedestrians: silver dial, self-winding" or the benefits of "A perfect folding Turkish bath." There's the Ashantee Pocket Hammock, of which Mr. H.M. Stanley of African renown says, "Nothing more portable yet so efficient and perfect for its purpose could be invented or manufactured," and the Gladstone bag, double-strapped against the suspect foreign porter.

several two-month excursions that concentrated purely on Egypt and the Nile. In all there were four steamer trips up the Nile that spring, conveying a total of 130 passengers.

Until this point the company was operating just two boats, but for the season 1872–73 the Egyptian administration agreed to provide four small steamers and one large, the *Beherah*. For its part, Cook & Son would oversee the procuring and provisioning of passengers and the running of the services, with the government taking a share of the revenues, with a guaranteed minimum payment. John scheduled more frequent departures, with a steamer leaving Cairo every other week from mid-November until the close of the season in March. To assist in managing the Nile services he appointed an agent, Robert Etzensberger, proprietor of the Hotel Victoria in Venice and the man who had provisioned the two steamers on the company's very first Nile tour in 1869. He was to spend the season in Egypt on Cook's behalf.

Aiding Cook & Son in their ability to fill the greatly increased number of Nile services was the fact that since the opening of the Suez Canal there were many more steamers calling at Egyptian ports en route to India and the Far East—until very recently these ships would have had to go around the Cape of Africa. By the early 1870s tourists had a multitude of options when it came to crossing the Mediterranean to either Alexandria or Port Said: Austrian Lloyd sailed from Trieste, Venice, and Brindisi; P&O ran steamers from Venice, Ancona, and Brindisi; the Rubattino Company from Genoa, Livorno, and Naples; Messageries Maritimes from Marseilles and Naples; and the Russian Company of Commerce and Navigation from the Black Sea and Constantinople.

Cook & Son's tourists would now be met at Alexandria and Port Said by boatmen, dressed in scarlet jackets with "Cook's Tours" sewn in white letters on the breast. Almost every traveler since the French army departed had written of the pandemonium that greeted any newly arrived ship as porters and touts threw themselves on visitors' luggage in a no-holds-barred scrimmage for baksheesh. Now, Cook's agents calmly took possession of passengers and baggage, and escorted them to the customs house. There, another set of porters in blue jackets, with those same white letters on their breast, would supervise transfer to the Cairo train.

For those booked on a Cook's steamer, the supplement for the twenty-day cruise to Aswan and back was now £44, a sum that covered everything including food, guides, donkeys to visit the monuments, small boats across the Nile where necessary, and candles for illumination in tombs. Not

ABOVE Navigazione Generale Italiana was an Italian shipping company formed in 1881 by the merger of Florio of Palermo and Rubattino of Genoa. Both companies operated extensively in the Mediterranean

OPPOSITE Founded in 1857, Bremen-based Norddeutscher Lloyd had become the world's second biggest shipping line, after P&O, by the end of the century. It launched routes to the Far East via Suez in 1886, and from Marseilles to Naples and Alexandria in 1904

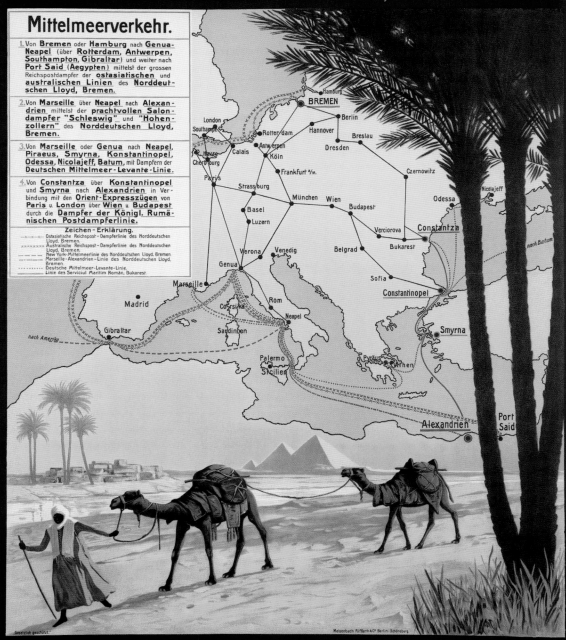

COMPAGNIE DES MESSAGERIES MARITIMES
Paquebots-Poste Français
Méditerranée, Mer Noire, Indo-Chine, Chine, Japon, Australie, Nouvelle-Calédonie, Côte Orientale d'Afrique, Madagascar, Espagne, Portugal, Sénégal, Brésil, La Plata.

Messageries Maritimes was a French shipping company that from its founding in 1851 operated routes from Marseilles to Egypt and the Middle East. These were later extended via the Suez Canal to the Indian Ocean and Far East, where it had a major base in Saigon

drink, though—Thomas and John remained united in their disapproval of alcohol, although they were not above selling it to passengers for an additional fee.

Steamer passengers would spend all twenty nights aboard their boat—there weren't, in fact, any hotels upriver at this time—but in Cairo, prior to boarding, they would generally be booked into Shepheard's. Of the city's handful of hotels, it was possibly the best known, at least to English travelers (founder Samuel Shepheard had been an Englishman, although he had sold up and quit Egypt in 1860). Two other hotels, the Orient and du Nil, were favored by the French for their authentic 'oriental' atmosphere—the du Nil, particularly, was a converted Arab merchant's house complete with *mashrabiya* screens and a courtyard garden buried deep in the suqs. Shepheard's was in the new, European part of the city. Théophile Gautier, who was lodged at Shepheard's as a guest of Egypt for the Suez Canal celebrations, was not impressed: "From the outside a large, bare and austere building, more like an English barracks than an Eastern caravanserai, and inside like a great monastery with half-lit stairways and bed-rooms like monastic cells." But the place suited Cook & Son. It was connected by wide boulevards to both the main railway station and the quayside where the company's steamers moored.

Etzensberger used Shepheard's as his office, an arrangement that was formalized in 1873 when Cook & Son took over a pavilion in the hotel grounds; the company would maintain its office at Shepheard's, moving up the street with the hotel to new premises in 1890, until both were burnt down in anti-British riots in 1952. Etzensberger was gone well before then, before the end of 1873, in fact, lured away to England to manage the newly opened Midland Grand Hotel at St. Pancras in London.

Meanwhile, there continued to be visitors to Egypt of maybe a more romantic disposition—certainly with a fuller bank account—who preferred to do their traveling independently and free of schedules, and who still chose to do the Nile by *dahabiya*. Thanks to the success of her *A Thousand Miles up the Nile*, the most renowned of these remains Amelia Edwards. When she set out on the river in the winter of 1873, it was only three years since John Cook had established a regular steamer service, but already a certain amount of snobbery is apparent, as Edwards noted how at dinner at Shepheard's it was possible to distinguish at first sight between a Cook's tourist and an independent traveler.★

Cook & Son felt compelled to defend its enterprise. In the 20 July 1872 edition of the *Excursionist*, the company's in-house journal, Thomas forcefully, and with only the slightest exaggeration, enumerated the advantages of the steamer over the *dahabiya*. The theme was taken up at greater length in a slim volume entitled *Up the Nile by Steam*, published in 1872, by Cook & Son, and penned by Cairo agent Etzensberger.

Nothing has probably been so fully described and praised to exhaustion as the famous *dahabiya* and the idyllic charms of life in one of these boats, floating up and down the Nile. No doubt, for a party of very dear friends on a shooting excursion, a young couple in their honeymoon, invalids in search of health, young swells who have nothing at all to do on Earth but kill time and throw away their money—in fact, for any one who can easily shut himself out from

---

★ On the pecking order of Nile travel, Edwards wrote, "The people in dahabeeyahs [*dahabiya*s] despise Cook's tourists; those who are bound for the Second Cataract look down with lofty compassion on those whose ambition extends only to the First; and travellers who engage their boat by the month hold their heads a little higher than those who contract for the trip."

all communication with the civilized world, and has got the temper to lie idle for weeks and months, looking every day on the same uniformly desolate scenery, nothing can be more delicious: besides, it is 'the Fashion'. Who would dare to confess, in good society, to having been up the Nile, except by *dahabiya*?

From light ridicule, we progress to severe peril …

Such small drawbacks as sudden severe illness, accidents from fire-arms, and consequent helplessness of the travelers—no medical aid being obtainable—even deaths on board, occurring every season, are never even mentioned but those who have witnessed this, and have seen those unfortunate parties return, and heard their tale of woe, know better. During last season, 1871–2, several sad incidents happened, and frequently the steamers were hailed for medical assistance from the ship's doctor, or to take in tow *dahabiya*s wanting to return as fast as possible to Cairo. Unfortunately, towing of any craft is strictly prohibited, and these applications had all to be declined.

… followed by admonishments against inadvertent slavery …

A *dahabiya*, when becalmed, may be detained in the same spot for a whole week; or, if the passengers insist, as they must do if they want

PREVIOUS SPREAD Cook & Son tourists pose in front of the temple of Karnak sometime in the late nineteenth century. On the far right, in buttoned coat and hat, is Cook's representative, while at far left, leaning against a column, is a member of the crew from the boat

BELOW Founded by an Englishman, after whom the place was named, Shepheard's hotel in Cairo was traditionally favored by the British, initially officers and civil servants traveling overland to and from imperial service in India, later by the likes of Thomas Cook and his tour parties

to move on, and there is no head wind, the crew will work away and haul the boat up stream—very painful sight, and really galley work. Look at those poor fellows yoked together with a rope round their breasts, toiling along with outstretched and swollen necks, and listen to their painful song as they work, slowly advancing, by short steps, at the rate of from five to six miles per day!

… and to top it all, falling out with friends and peers.

It very frequently happens that a party for a *dahabiya* is only made up in Cairo, between people who never knew or met each other before. On starting, it is soon found out that their characters are anything but congenial; angry word produces another, and after a few days serious quarrelling breaks out. If these parties are still within the reach of the Railway, they break up and return to Cairo; if beyond, they have to endure each other's society until the end of the voyage.

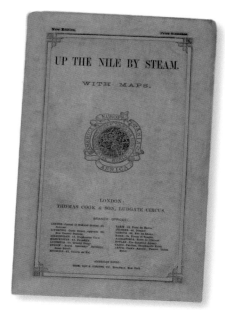

Etzensberger, an employee of Cook & Son, wrote *Up the Nile by Steam* as a riposte to the genre of books written by travelers who felt bound after a *dahabiya* trip to publish their "generally very uninteresting" personal accounts

In contrast, argued Etzensberger, the Nile steamers, which at the time generally carried from twelve to twenty passengers, were full of what he characterizes as "well-educated and nice people," who behaved to each other "with due regard, became fast friends and delighted each other with their knowledge and reading." And if people did not get on, well, while that can be bad aboard a steamer, he says, "it is ten times worse in a *dahabiya*" where one runs the risk of spending "three miserable months with disagreeable travelling companions instead of so many weeks."

What's more, doing the Nile by *dahabiya*, according to Etzensberger, meant that travelers experienced Egypt in completely the wrong order. The need to make the most of the winds typically meant sailing non-stop to Aswan where the sightseeing would begin, then working back north toward Cairo. By contrast, he maintained, the order of sightseeing by steamer was in harmony with the importance of the monuments, progressing from minor sights such as the tombs of Beni Hasan to the more impressive temple of Dendara, then the splendors of Luxor, and finally the incomparable Philae and Abu Simbel.

Other opinions, of course, were available. The redoubtable Amelia Edwards, for instance, could not have disagreed more: "The choice between dahabeeyah and steamer is like the choice between travelling with post-horses and travelling by rail. The one is expensive, leisurely, and delightful; the other is cheap, swift and comfortless. Those who are content to snatch but a glimpse of the Nile will doubtless prefer the steamer."★ American journalist Charles Dudley Warner condemned the "miserable steamboats" for "frightening all the game birds, and fouling the sweet air of Egypt with the black smoke of their chimneys."

Still, plenty were content to "snatch but a glimpse" because with each successive season Nile bookings for Cook & Son were up. In advance of the 1874–75 season, the company took note of criticisms made by passengers of the quality of the boats and had them remodeled to include deck saloons for viewing and new kitchens shipped in from England. A notice of the work appeared in the September 1875 issue of the *Excursionist* announcing that under the control of Cook & Son, the Nile steamers had met with the general satisfaction of "princes, dukes and commoners"—although who the princes and dukes were it didn't say. The same issue was also pleased to announce the extension of the existing Nile service beyond Aswan, where the boats currently terminated, and on to Wadi Halfa and the Second Cataract—but more of that later.

Cook & Son was really quite pleased with itself and its rapidly expanding Egyptian business, which with the increasing political involvement of England in Egypt could only grow. Owing to the bankruptcy of Khedive Ismail, the British prime minister Benjamin Disraeli had been able to purchase, in November 1875, a controlling interest in the Suez Canal Company, prompting Thomas to write in the following month's *Excursionist* that he would be glad to take a commission under Disraeli to provide a Suez Canal steamboat service:

> If Ismailia were on the Thames, instead of on Lake Timsah, it would soon be raised to the dignity of a popular winter health resort. If a party of English ladies and gentlemen wish to go out and see the 'purchased possession,' we will take them there and back, and give them a trip to the Pyramids into the bargain, for fifty guineas. Mr. John M. Cook would be glad to have their company. . . . Who'll go?"

Nothing came of the proposed Suez service, but Cook & Son's operations in Egypt were developed in another significant way around this time with

---

★ Cook & Son was able to engage in a bit of score settling in 1877 when Edwards' newly published *A Thousand Miles up the Nile* came to be reviewed in the *Excursionist*. "There are one or two points in the present volume upon which our experience has carried us somewhat further than the author's," it stated a bit sniffily. The review took exception to Edwards's dismissal of steamers as "comfortless," saying

the company's first venture into the land-based hospitality business. Its Luxor hotel was the first hotel in Upper Egypt—until this time, if you did not have the luxury of your own *dahabiya*, the only other options had been to occupy a chamber in the main pylon at Karnak temple (not very comfortable, said Murray's 1867 guide), or possibly a tomb over on the east bank. Rather than build from scratch, which would have occasioned an expense possibly not warranted given the current level of business, John found a modern house of a reasonable size, surrounded by five feddans of land, and bought it. During the summer of 1877, he expanded the property so that it now had twenty-three bedrooms. The hotel opened for the beginning of the 1877–78 season, and immediately proved so popular that the next summer a new wing was added, doubling the number of beds.

Already, in 1860–61, the author of *Four Months in a Dahabëéh* was complaining she could not make out wall paintings at Philae because previous travelers had blackened them with smoke from their torches and fires. Later guidebooks would recommend magnesium wire and a lamp for burning it in as the proper way to light dark temple and tomb interiors

---

if that was the case then why were the services all overbooked? It suggested Edwards was insufficiently observant and that her book was out of date, being based on a trip made four years previously. The reviewer damned it with faint praise, suggesting the book was "well adapted for the drawing-room table"—the implication being it wasn't worth having along in Egypt.

This was significant: steamers halted at Luxor for three days before moving on. Now, tourists had the option of disembarking, checking into the new hotel, and picking up another steamer a fortnight or even a month hence. At this time Luxor was no more than a cluster of mud-brick residences in and around the ruins of the riverside Luxor Temple, which were at this time still largely buried beneath mounded sand. That same Murray's guide offers no description of the village, and suggests visitors might equally well moor on either side of the river. Just ten years later, the 1888 edition of Murray's is describing Luxor as a "large village of 3,600 inhabitants, increasing both in population and prosperity." In addition to the "excellent hotel," it has a post office with a postmaster who speaks English fluently, as well as a telegraph office, and shops for provisions.

Remarkably detailed information on Cook's Nile steamer service for the first half of the 1878–79 season survives thanks to the *Moniteur Egyptien*, the official organ of the Egyptian government. It records that on the first sailing of that season, on 10 December 1878, the boat *Beherah* left Qasr al-Nil bridge in Cairo with eighteen English, eighteen Americans, three Italians, and two Chileans onboard, making a total of forty-one passengers, of whom nineteen were bound for the First Cataract and back, eleven for the Second Cataract, and eleven were breaking their stay at the Luxor Hotel. On 24 December, the *Mehallah* set sail with twenty English, six Americans, four French, five Germans, two Austrians, and one Dutchman,

A rare photograph of early steamers on the Nile, circa 1867. These are possibly some of the boats hired by Cook & Son from the khedive, who would not allow any other steamers than his own on the river. They were originally little more than cargo boats and quite uncomfortable

with eleven for the First Cataract only, thirteen for the Second Cataract, and fourteen staying at the Luxor Hotel.

The *Beherah* sailed again from Cairo on 7 January 1879 with forty-two passengers, and the *Mehallah* made its second sailing two weeks later with thirty-seven paying guests. "The first four ships of the season have thus carried the important number of 158 passengers," reported the newspaper, "amongst whom figure the nobility of every country."

Although business in Egypt was excellent, things were less rosy between Thomas Cook and son, who continued to clash. For example, on returning from his round-the-world tour Thomas refused to set foot in the company's grand new London headquarters at Ludgate Circus, which John had purchased with a loan and which Thomas considered grossly extravagant. In return, John accused Thomas of making a string of bad business decisions and bringing ruination on the company (Thomas stubbornly persisted in championing an American partner who was at best incompetent if not an outright crook). Thomas insinuated that John was misappropriating the firm's funds for his own benefit. The feuding continued throughout the 1870s and the eventual upshot was that Thomas was forced out of the company he founded. In 1879, at the age of 71, he reluctantly gave in to his son's demands and went into retirement, returning to Leicester where he busied himself with temperance and missionary work on a pension of £1,000 a year, plus free travel. John became the company's sole managing partner.

From contemporary accounts, John sounds quite intimidating: he was tall and heavily built—"an iron will in an iron frame"—with "eyes that look out of their sockets like a gun out of a port." Whereas his father was renowned for his good humor and forbearance, playing tutor, counselor, and nursemaid to the members of his tour parties, John was not a patient man: one commentator reckoned his baldness had been caused by his exasperation at having to play tour guide. He had a temper, which on one occasion led him to throw a disobedient dragoman into the Nile; on another trip he ended an argument with a steamboat captain in a similar manner. A lady resident of Egypt who knew John Cook, and twice traveled on the Nile with him, called him a dictator. She broke her leg at Karnak, which made John Cook angry because it fouled up his plans. On another voyage the steamer was delayed by getting stuck on a sandbank and arrived too late in the day to pass through the Asyut barrage. John asked the Scottish engineer in charge to open the gates for him and was refused. There was a row in which the engineer declared that he "would

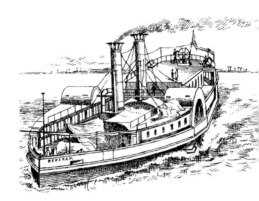

Possibly the only existing image of the *Beherah*, one of the khedive's boats used by Cook & Son. This drawing was used in the company's advertising for its "Steam Navigation on the Nile" services in the late 1870s and early 1880s

A portrait of John Mason Cook, who after 1871 ran the company's operations in Egypt, spending every winter there from 1885 onward

not open the barrage again that day for God Almighty Himself." "He'll open it for me," swore Cook, dispatching a telegram to Cairo. And the engineer did.★

But if he was a despot, he was a benevolent despot. He gave generously to charities and inspired loyalty in his employees and friends. In Luxor, where locals had got into the habit of bringing the sick to the steamers to ask for medical help, he funded the construction of a hospital, the first in Upper Egypt, and covered the annual running costs.

Khedive Ismail was deposed in June 1879, accompanied by an entire change of the cabinet, but when Cook & Son's ten-year contract for the operation of the Nile steamer service was up in July 1880, there was probably no hesitation from either side over its renewal.

The document, signed by John's manager of the steamboat services, a Greek by the name of Alexander Rostovitz, and the Egyptian minister for public works, Ali Pasha Mubarak, extended Cook & Son's monopoly on the Nile for a further ten years. It granted the company the exclusive use of the government steamers *Beherah*, *Beniswaif*, *Jasrieh*, *Mahmoudieh*, *Mehallah*, and *Nil*, along with a new boat, the *Masr*. This latter steamer was the largest on the Nile, and had previously been used to carry troops in Abyssinia (which Egypt had invaded in October 1875); Cook & Son stripped it down to the hull and refitted it for passenger use at the company's expense, creating accommodation for sixty in thirty single-berth cabins and fifteen double-berth. The work was completed in just four months, with the *Masr*'s inaugural passenger voyage taking place on 1 February 1881, when she sailed carrying the largest number of passengers that had until this time gone up the Nile.

Significantly, the independent travel company of Cook & Son was also given the license to run the official Khedivial Mail Service on the Nile. This entailed running express steamers between Asyut (as far south as the Cairo railway went) and Aswan connecting the towns and villages of Upper Egypt; these boats were also provisioned with a number of first-class cabins for paying passengers. Thomas Cook & Son had an absolute monopoly on the Nile.

The *dahabiya* business was still holding up despite competition from the steamers, and so Cook & Son decided it might as well have a piece: it acquired some of the better sailboats on the river, and built one of its own,

★ This story comes from Mabel Caillard's *A Lifetime in Egypt*, and while it illustrates just how bloody-minded John Mason Cook could be, it is rendered slightly suspect by the knowledge that the Asyut barrage was not actually completed until four years after his death.

which was called the *Philites*. In fact, Etzensberger's booklet *Up the Nile by Steam*, which since 1875 had been reissued each season with updated information on the steamer services, was renamed in 1880 *Up the Nile by Khedive Steamers and by Dahabeah*.

The stipulations of the new steamer-service contract were very exact: sailors, officers, and captains on the boats were to be provided by the government; chefs, waiters, and other non-technical crew by Cook & Son. For each passenger conveyed from Cairo to Aswan and back, Cook & Son had to pay the ministry 1,600 piasters. Said passengers were to be provided with food "which must be of the best quality," and served as follows: at 8:30 a.m. coffee or tea and milk, biscuits, jam, honey, butter, and one hot dish; at noon a lunch composed of three hors d'oeuvres, two entrees, two vegetables, one pastry, fine bread, and coffee; at 6 p.m. dinner composed of four hors d'oeuvres, two entrees, two vegetables, two grilled or roast meats, two desserts, four fruits, bread, and coffee; and at 9 p.m. tea, milk, and biscuits. A book was to be put at the disposal of the passengers for the registering of complaints and on each boat's return to Cairo the book had to be presented to the ministry for inspection; serious complaints could draw a fine of up to £70 and if the total amount of fines in one season exceeded £350 then the government was at liberty to terminate the contract.

As it happened, the contract was voided halfway through the term, but neither Cook & Son nor the Egyptian government was to blame.

COOK GOES TO WAR

"Egypt is now in the hands of two armies of occupation. One is composed of British soldiers, and the other of the men of Thomas Cook & Son." SIR GEORGE NEWNES, 1899

When Thomas Cook took his first party of tourists up the Nile in 1869, the farthest south the steamers sailed was Aswan. There was a good reason for this: at Aswan hard granite rocks poked up through the silty bed of the river to create four miles of boulder-filled shallows, islets, and gorges. Around these the currents quickened and the water churned into fast-flowing rapids that made passage treacherous for all but the smallest, most nimble boats. This was the First Cataract; there was a Second Cataract 210 miles to the south at Wadi Halfa, and a further four, similarly rocky sections obstructing passage on the way to Khartoum.

The First Cataract was the natural boundary of Egypt and marked the division with the territory of Nubia, which lay between the first two cataracts, and beyond that, Sudan. This desert region was under the control of Egypt, conquered in 1820 by Muhammad Ali in order to harvest its primary resource: slaves. The most powerful of ancient Egypt's pharaonic rulers had done the same, extending their rule south of the First Cataract, and Nubia was studded with the temples and monuments they built, including two that have always been rhapsodized by foreign visitors.

The first of these was Philae, with its island temple sacred to Isis. This was easily visited from Aswan; Nile travelers could moor their *dahabiya*s north of the First Cataract and bypass the rapids on land. A ride of about an hour and a half on a donkey took them south out of town and across the scrubby desert to the river moorings at Shellal, where small boats waited to ferry tourists the short distance to the island. Passengers on Cook's steamers could also follow this route, making Philae an easy day's excursion from Aswan.

The second Nubian site that all travelers aimed to see could not be reached from Aswan, not by land. The imposing temple of Abu Simbel, with its façade of four colossal seated statues of Ramesses II, lay 175 miles south, with no road or trail to follow, only a blankness of desert sand.

Determined travelers with their own *dahabiya* could apply to the "Sheikh of the Cataract," who, for a not insubstantial sum, could have a boat hauled

OPPOSITE Soldiers taking part in the Gordon Relief Expedition of 1884 make their way upriver in the small boats known as "whalers"

The First Cataract at Aswan, where the water rushed and swirled around boulders and islets, and presented an obstacle to progress south

through the rapids. This involved a small army of pilots, perhaps as many as two hundred, maneuvering the boat with ropes from the shore, with poles wielded onboard, and with the muscle of their arms as they swam in the river alongside.

The American lawyer-turned-journalist William Cowper Prime hired the services of the sheikh in 1855 to get his rented boat, the *Phantom*, through the cataract. After stowing away all glass and loose objects, and lashing down the furniture, they maneuvered into the rapids. For two miles they managed to navigate dashing waters, skirting rocks, sliding with a grating jar over smooth stones that lay hidden under the boiling foam, until the current became so fierce that even with the wind in their sails the boat could not move forward.

The [sheikh] watched the full and straining sail; and as he saw her slowly yield and give back to the heavy rush of the river, he shouted for a rope, and, seizing the coils, dropped his turban and all his clothes, quick as lightning, and sprang into the furious current. Ten strokes of his powerful arms, and he was on a black rock, around which the water was raging. From this he dived again, up stream, and disappeared. The next instant he came above water, far up stream. No human power could swim that distance in that current. He had, doubtless, helped himself along by rocks on the bottom of the stream; but he had never let go his hold on the heavy rope. A dozen Nubians

This was a statement slightly at odds with the facts, given that 31,000 British troops from Malta, Cyprus, and India had been landed in Egypt two months previously with the aim of restoring the rule of the khedive and protecting Britain's financial interests, primarily the Suez Canal. Under the command of General Sir Garnet Wolseley, the British had engaged and defeated the forces of 'Urabi at the battle of Tell al-Kebir. Since that time, Egypt was under the occupation of the British Army.

Despite the pro-Egyptian sentiments of John's editorial, Cook & Son was a British company, largely serving the interests of British travelers, and heavily reliant on British custom for its continued profitability. So it was that following the fighting, Cook & Son transported wounded and sick British soldiers from Cairo to Alexandria for evacuation home. It stationed one of its *dahabiya*s on the Sweet-Water Canal at Tell al-Kebir to serve as a hotel for battlefield tourists, and arranged pleasure cruises for Wolseley and his staff, and for convalescing soldiers. Members of the British press were invited along to make sure the company's munificence didn't go unreported. Gratitude was expressed at the highest levels.

War Office, Pall Mall
8th February 1883

GENTLEMEN,—The Lieutenant-General commanding the
troops in Egypt having forwarded, for the information of the Field
Marshal the Commander-in-Chief, a report of the cordial assistance
rendered by your firm in conveying convalescents for sanitary
reasons in your steamers on the Nile, I have now the honour, by
desire of His Royal Highness, to convey to you an expression of
his thanks for the admirable arrangements made by you on these
occasions, by which the troops have greatly benefitted.

Your obedient servant,

ARTHUR HERBERT
Lt.-General, Quartermaster-General

The following year, the relationship between Cook & Son and the British Army was drawn even closer. In November 1883, the Mahdi, a self-styled new prophet of Islam intent on leading a holy war against infidels in Sudan, annihilated a British-led Egyptian army that had been dispatched

Whalers being offloaded from barges at Elephantine Island, Aswan. The British weekly journal *The Illustrated London News* sent writers and artists on the Gordon Relief Expedition and covered its progress extensively

from Khartoum to reassert imperial order. This left the Sudanese capital vulnerable to attack, with its six thousand poorly trained, largely leaderless Egyptian troops, as well as government officials and their families. After much debate, the British government decided to dispatch a small expedition to organize the evacuation of Khartoum. The man selected for the job was General Charles Gordon, who had fought in the Crimea in 1854 and in China in 1860, and who more recently served as the governor-general of Sudan under Khedive Ismail. He was regarded by many as the British Empire's top soldier, the "greatest and best man of this century," in the words of *The Times* of London's war correspondent, Frank Power. When Gordon and his modest entourage set off from Asyut for Khartoum, it was in a Cook & Son steamer.

He was conveyed to Aswan and then on to Korosko, midway between the First and Second Cataracts, from where the expedition set out south across the Nubian Desert. Before breaking camp Gordon sent a letter of thanks to Cook & Son.

Korosko
1st February 1884

GENTLEMEN,—Before leaving for Berber I would wish to express to you my own and Lieut.-Colonel Stewart's thanks for the admirable manner in which we have been treated while on your steamers. Your agents have also on every occasion shown themselves kind and obliging, and have in every way assisted us to the best of their ability. Hoping that I may perhaps have again the pleasure of placing myself under your guidance, I remain, ever yours truly,

C.E. Gordon,
Major-General and Governor-General

Once at Khartoum, the mission began well enough, with the evacuation of around 2,500 women, children, sick, and wounded. However, Gordon's position became rapidly more precarious as the weeks went by and it became clear to the city's inhabitants that no great rescue force was coming. Khartoum's previously loyal but self-preservationist Sudanese began to transfer their support to the Mahdist army, now laying siege from its encampment just over the Nile at Omdurman.

After months of prevarication, and faced with the outrage of the British public at the seeming abandonment of one of its greatest heroes, the British government finally determined to take steps to reinforce Gordon. General Wolseley was tasked with heading up what would become known as the Gordon Relief Expedition. The rescue plan he came up with involved ferrying an army 1,060 miles from Cairo to Khartoum, for the most part on the Nile. In summer 1884, Cook & Son was requested to hold all passenger steamer activity and reserve its fleet for possible use by the British Army. For the first time in fifteen years Cook & Son was not able to advertise a tourist service on the Nile for the coming season.

On 2 September, John received official written confirmation that he was to assist in moving 6,000 men, and between 6,000 and 8,000 tons of stores, from Asyut up to Wadi Halfa at the foot of the Second Cataract. To assist in this, Wolseley was supplying 400 light boats, known as whalers, which had been hastily built in England, shipped to Alexandria, and sent to Asyut by train, where they were to be filled with soldiers and supplies; from here they were to be towed in strings behind Cook's steamers. Once at Wadi Halfa, the Relief Expedition would continue on in two columns, one on the river, one overland across the desert. The river column would utilize the whalers, which were small and mobile enough to negotiate the cataracts or, alternatively, be carried over the sand and then relaunched.

In fact, over the next two months, Cook & Son transported far in excess of the original contract, to the tune of 18,000 troops and 40,000 tons of

British soldiers being ferried up the Nile on a requisitioned steamer cheer General Wolseley, leader of the expedition to rescue Gordon in Khartoum

PREVIOUS SPREAD British soldiers and Sudanese natives attempt to haul a steamer through one of the six cataracts that lay between Aswan and Gordon in Khartoum

ABOVE But not every steamer made it through successfully

stores, conveyed by 800 whalers. The project required the use of twenty-seven steamers and 650 sailing boats, and a private Cook's army of 5,000 men, mostly Egyptian peasantry. This is believed to be the only occasion on which the British Army has gone to war conveyed by private transport.

Again, Cook was praised at the highest levels. There were, however, dissenting voices, notably Lord Charles Beresford, a member of Wolseley's staff, who published an opinionated and self-serving autobiography thirty years after the event, in which he had plenty to say about Cook's boats:

I left Assiout [Asyut] in one of Messrs. Cook's steamers, the *Fersaat*, which had the appearance of a boat and the manners of a kangaroo. She was loosely concocted of iron and leaked at every rivet; she squealed and grunted; her boiler roared like a camel; she bounded as she went. Her Reis (captain and pilot) was a sorrowful old Muhammedan, whose only method of finding out if the shoals and sands were still in the same place was by running upon them; and his manner of getting off them was to cry "Allah Kerim!" ("God is great!") and to beat his poor old forehead on the deck. In the meantime one of his Arabs, tastefully attired in a long blue night-gown, an enormous pair of drawers, and decorated elastic-sided boots, stripped and jumped overboard and pushed the boat, and while he pushed he chanted a dirge. As the boat began to move, he made sounds which suggested that he was about to be violently sick but could not quite manage it satisfactorily. When he clambered back on deck, he put on the decorated boots and walked about in them till he was dry enough to dress; while the Reis gave thanks to his Maker.

If anyone walked from port to starboard or touched the helm, the boat rolled over, and until the next roll maintained a list of ten degrees, so that I was frequently shot off the locker upon which I was trying to sleep, landing upon the top of José, my Maltese interpreter, and followed by field-glasses, filter, sword and boots. The mosquito-curtains carried away, and the mosquitoes instantly attacked in force, driving me nearly mad with loss of blood, irritation, and rage. My only comfort was a pneumatic life-belt, which had been sent to me by Lady Charles, and which I used as a pillow.

Lord Beresford set up camp at Wadi Halfa, where he occupied a small tent furnished with a penny whistle, a photograph of Lady Charles, his letters from home, and a stag beetle big enough "to carry me to hounds." Here, at the Second Cataract, the Nile divided into two, flowing on either side of a group of rocks and islands for about twenty miles, before charging in a tremendous rush through the sickle-shaped gorge of Bab al-Kebir, the 'Great Gate.' Lord Wolseley suspected it would be impossible to get the steamers through but Beresford, who was tasked with assessing the job, responded that he would admit the impossibility only when he'd smashed two steamers trying. Some 4,000 men hauled ropes in the attempt to get a first steamer through. In places there was no more than a few inches of clearance between its sides and the rocks, and the torrent flung the boat against them; if it hadn't been padded with timber and mats it would have been smashed to pieces. The boats eventually all got through but it was necessary to establish a dockyard south of the cataract for the repair of damaged boats.

John accompanied the fleet as far south as Dongola, which was some 250 miles south of Wadi Halfa. Possibly he wanted to keep an eye on his boats, or perhaps he was scouting out the possibilities of extending the company's operation into Sudan. With him was his youngest son, Bert, seventeen at the time but already as tall and broad as his father. Together, they traveled in a *dahabiya* rented from a local Sudanese dignitary, only twenty-four foot in length with cabin ceilings of five foot six; they called it the Dog House. The sailing was rough going, with John claiming twenty holes were knocked in the boat at one cataract alone; the vessel had to be taken out of the water on several occasions for hasty repairs. In fact, it generally wasn't possible to

Supply camels being ferried across the Nile at Dongola in Sudan

The Tragedy of the Korosko

Two years after killing off Sherlock Holmes in *The Final Problem*, his creator Arthur Conan Doyle, in the company of wife and sister, spent the winter of 1895–96 in Egypt. Arthur had a fascination for the place—in two short stories of the supernatural, "The Ring of Thoth" (published 1890) and "Lot No. 249" (1892), he had pretty much set the template for the mummy horror film—while his tubercular wife had been told by her doctor that time in a hot, dry country would do her good. The trio took up residence at the Mena House hotel beside the Pyramids, where Arthur wrote, climbed the Great Pyramid ("an uncomfortable and useless feat"), played golf, and practiced his horsemanship, not always successfully—one horse kicked him in the head, an injury that left him with a permanently droopy eyelid.

A few days after New Year in 1896, the Conan Doyles set off on a Nile cruise aboard the *Nitocris*, a small, private Cook & Son steamer, with berths for eight and a crew of sixteen. They traveled to Luxor and Aswan, and on beyond the First Cataract to Wadi Halfa. This was potentially dangerous territory. While the British government was debating reconquest, the Sudan remained in the hands of the Mahdists, and bands of tribesmen had been marauding along the Nubian stretch of the Nile. The *Nitocris* moored on 16 January at a village that had been the scene of a recent attack by dervishes, and Conan Doyle wrote in his diary, "If I were a Dervish general, I would undertake to carry off a Cook's excursion party with the greatest ease."

The Conan Doyle party returned to Cairo without incident, but the idea stuck with Arthur and not too long after provided the plot for a new short novel called *The Tragedy of the Korosko* (1898). In it, a party of tourists traveling on the fictional steamer *Korosko*, "a turtle-bottomed, round-bowed sternwheeler, with a 30-inch draught and the lines of a flat-iron," fall prey to desert bandits. The dervishes behead some of the tourists and plan to sell the women at Khartoum's slave market, but happily the British Army with its Egyptian allies arrive in time to save the day.

sail and for most of the journey the boat had to be hauled from the bank or propelled by poling. However, other than the small whalers, John and Bert's *dahabiya* was the only boat to reach Dongola, achieved in twenty-one days, and Lord Wolseley himself entertained the pair to dinner there.

John and Bert remained for just four days before returning north. They swapped the *dahabiya* for places in a whaler piloted by Canadian "voyageurs," some of four hundred native North American Indians that Wolseley, a veteran of campaigns in Canada, had brought over for their skill in handling small boats on rough river waters. Wolseley himself traveled at the head of his expeditionary fleet, often in a birch bark canoe rowed by Iroquois Indians. John reckoned the voyageurs were the finest boatmen he had ever come into contact with, and with one of them at the helm of a small whaler, one series of cataracts that had taken thirteen days coming up was completed in just eleven hours.

The mission to rescue Gordon was, of course, a failure, with the British arriving two days too late to save their fêted general. But Cook & Son came out of it well. More than one journalist expressed the opinion that if the travel company had been responsible for taking the expedition all the way to Khartoum, Gordon might well have been saved. As well as winning considerable acclaim for his company, John, ever the shrewd businessman, also made a very tidy profit from the operation. This led to some resentment from the military chiefs in charge of the failed operation, including Wolseley.

One of the greatest matters of contention was the issue of who was responsible for the destructive wear and tear suffered by the steamers. At the end of the campaign they had been left totally unfit to put back into passenger service. Another tourist season was now to be a complete write-off because, bar some *dahabiya*s and the odd small steamer, the company had no serviceable boats.

John's solution was typically ambitious: he decided to build a Nile fleet of his own. Thomas Cook & Son's new steamers, he announced, "will be floating palaces and will be finer than anything that has floated on the grand old river since the days of Cleopatra."

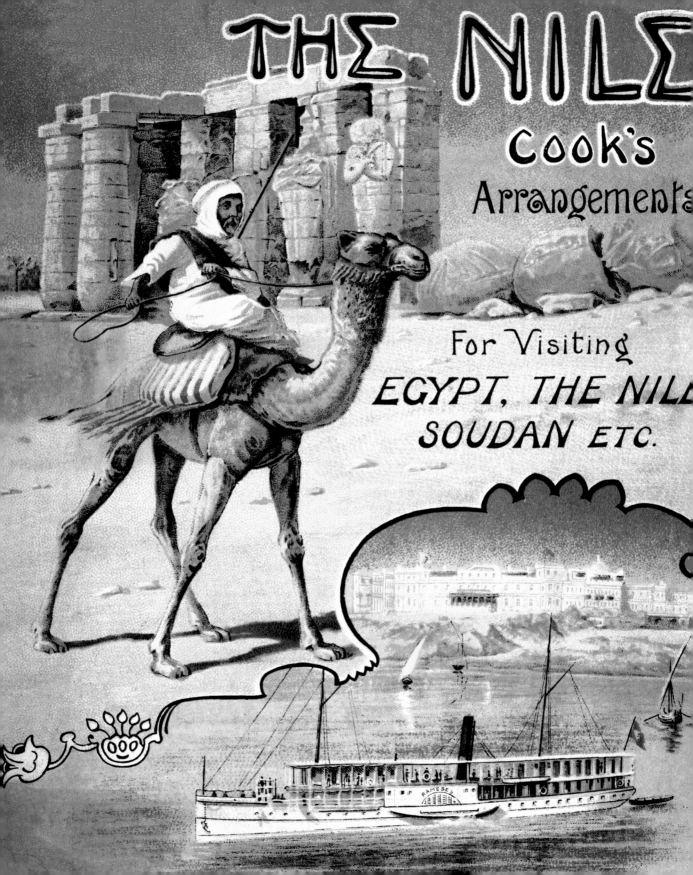

FLOATING PALACES

"Once in a way one of Cook's tourist steamers comes merrily up from Cairo—a thing of beauty, with its gleaming white hull and its decks as gay as a garden party." DOUGLAS SLADEN, 1908

In 1888 Cook & Son's seasonal "Egypt and the Nile" brochure opened with an apology of sorts: "It will be known to all who have watched the course of events in Egypt, that from the season 1883–84 until the past season of 1886–87, we have not been in the position to justify us announcing a regular tourist steamboat service on the Nile."

By 1888 that position had most definitely changed. Not only had regular services resumed, but they were being operated by a completely new, purpose-built fleet of Cook & Son paddle steamers, built to order and custom-fitted for Nile service.

Paddle steamers were the first powered vessels—that is, the first boats not reliant on the wind and sails. Experiments in fitting a steam-engine in a hull had been tried out as early as the 1780s, but the first commercially functioning boat to sail under steam ran on the Hudson River in New York in September 1807. A few years later, the Scotsman Henry Bell had the *Comet* running regular services on the Clyde in Scotland, while the first transatlantic crossing by a steamship (actually a converted sailing ship) took place in 1819. Within twenty years there were paddle steamers operating on major rivers and sea routes across Europe and America.

It is thought the steamship made its debut appearance on the Nile in or around May 1837, when Laird, Son & Co. of Birkenhead, England, delivered an iron steam yacht to Muhammad Ali, which was named *l'Egyptienne*. By 1844, the Viceroy's river steamer fleet had been expanded to five vessels (he also had three much larger seagoing steamers, part of a powerful, if ramshackle, navy being gathered for use in campaigns in Arabia). In addition, from 1840, the London-based P&O Steam Navigation Company was operating three steamers, the *Cairo*, *Little Nile*, and *Lotus*, on the Rosetta branch of the Nile between Atfih (near Alexandria) and Cairo, one short leg in a long-distance mail route between England and India that used overland travel across Egypt as an alternative to sailing around the tip of Africa. None of these, however, took passengers farther up the Nile than Cairo.

OPPOSITE The cover of Thomas Cook & Son's "Egypt & the Nile" brochure for 1904; the twenty years prior to this were probably the most significant period in the company's history in Egypt

Mail and passengers arrive at Alexandria, en route between Britain and India; they connected to Cairo by boat and to Suez by camel caravan, hence the service was known as the Overland Route

That had to wait until 1851, when Abbas Pasha, grandson of Muhammad Ali, inaugurated a monthly service of steamers between Cairo and Aswan. According to *The Oriental Pocket Companion* of 1852, these boats offered first-, second-, and deck-class passage. Meals were provided but not bedding and, in the case of accidental grounding, *passengers* would be liable to a surcharge for every twenty-four hours delayed. This does not seem to have been a particularly reliable operation: in 1861, French guidebook writer Adolphe Joanne was advising that it was no longer possible to take a steamer as the guild of Nile boatmen had forced the government to suspend services.

When it came to its new fleet, Cook & Son looked to Europe. The commission for the company's first two steamers was awarded to Fairfield Govan of Glasgow, on the Clyde River, a center of British shipbuilding for hundreds of years. The design of the boats was based on the American river steamers, with upper, main, and lower decks, and side-mounted paddlewheels. The hulls and superstructure were steel, with engines that gave a good speed but, at the same time, were economic in coal consumption. The boats were both 160 feet long by twenty feet wide, which made them bigger than anything that had previously worked the Nile. To minimize the risk of running aground, their draft (the depth between the waterline and the flat bottom of the hull) was just seven feet.

The completed hulls and engines were delivered in sections to Egypt in the second half of 1886, and assembled in Cairo. Here, Cook & Son had its own machine shops, fitters, and carpenters to complete the decks and cabins, and make the boats ready to receive passengers. An almost identical pair, the steamers were given the names *Tewfik*, in honor of the then khedive of Egypt, and *Prince Abbas*, after his eldest son. They made their trials on the Nile that October.

George Steevens, a correspondent with the British newspaper *The Daily Mail*, who became an enthusiastic cheerleader for John Mason Cook and his company after sailing with him in February 1898, claimed that the local captains were extremely dubious about the new steamers when they were unveiled at Cairo. They thought they would capsize in the first gale. The boats lay moored for days without setting out onto the river, which the skeptics took as evidence that their owner was as unsure as they were. But then on a day on which the wind was high and the river choppy, Cook ordered the *Prince Abbas* out. She was, reported Steevens, steady as a rock, and there was no more whispering about the stability of Cook's new Nile steamers after that.

On 29 November the *Prince Abbas* made another short sail, in this case just a mile upriver to moor beside the royal palace at Giza at the request of Khedive Tewfik. *The Egyptian Gazette* reported that His Highness was specially gratified to find that the new steamers were worked chiefly by Egyptians: the captains had actually been poached from government boats; the waiters for the saloon, attendants in the bedrooms, and other crew were all local, except for the men who tended the engines, who were Scottish.

The following morning at 10 a.m., the *Prince Abbas* set out on its maiden voyage up the Nile.★

That same day, 30 November 1886, a twenty-nine-year-old novice Egyptologist by the name of Wallis Budge stepped off the P&O steamship *Pekin* at Port Said. He had been sent by the trustees of the British Museum to excavate some Old and Middle Kingdom rock tombs at Aswan that had attracted the attention of General F.W. Grenfell, *sirdar* (commander) of the Egyptian Army, who had requested professional help in his treasure hunt. From Port Said Budge traveled down to Ismailiya, the nearest point on the

A letter to Cook & Son, written in 1891, from Bow McLachan & Co. of Paisley on the Clyde, who were the builders of the boilers and engines that were fitted in the early Nile steamers

---

★ New boats, but old prejudices remained. "The first of Cook's new steamers starts tomorrow for Assuan [Aswan]," wrote Charles Edwin Wilbour in November 1886. "I asked Mrs. Goadison, Ruskin's next door neighbour near Lake Windermere, why she did not go in it. She said, 'I could never face Mr. Ruskin [England's leading art critic] again if I were to go in a Cook boat.'" Ruskin, after all, is the man who, when the railway arrived in England, said, "Now every fool in Buxton can be in Bakewell in half an hour, and every fool in Bakewell in Buxton."

Cairo–Suez railway, where he boarded a train. Before he had even reached Cairo he'd made his first acquisitions of antiquities, in the form of some scarabs and small statuettes of the cat-headed goddess Bastet, bought from local peddlers who came aboard the train when it stopped near the site of the ancient city of Bubastis.

Once in Cairo Budge had a letter of introduction to the highest ranking colonial official in the country, Consul-General Sir Evelyn Baring, but it was a somewhat cool meeting, with Baring telling the Egyptologist that just because the British were in occupation of Egypt it didn't give them license to go filching the country's antiquities. Budge was puzzled by this attitude—after all, everybody else was doing it. After three days in Cairo, Budge joined the *sirdar*'s party on a train bound for Asyut; here they embarked on the "new and splendid passenger steamer, *Prince Abbas*," where they found John Mason Cook on board, personally directing her maiden voyage.

We continued our journey to Aswan on the 11th, and Mr. J.M. Cook made excellent arrangements for us to examine the temples of Edfu, Esna, and Kom Ombo, and in due course we arrived at Daraw. Here the crew dressed the steamer with hundreds of the gaudy flags, which are so dear to the heart of the Egyptian, and when we started again a large crowd of natives ran along the river bank waving flags, and shouting and beating little drums with appalling vigor. We steamed on quite slowly, accompanied by an awful noise from the bank, and as we neared the town we saw that almost every building was decorated with flags. When we passed the "North End" of Aswan, rifles were fired from the bank, and everyone afloat and ashore shouted and

PREVIOUS SPREAD The *Prince Abbas*, one of a pair of boats commissioned by Cook & Son to replace the steamers lost or irreparably damaged during the Gordon Relief Expedition, and introduced for the season 1886–87

BELOW The *Tewfik* made her maiden Nile passenger sailing on 15 November 1886, two weeks before her sister vessel, the *Prince Abbas*

screamed his loudest. All this noise was in honor of (1) the steamer, the largest which had ever been seen at Aswan, and the symbol of many tourists, and therefore of much baksheesh; (2) Mr. J.M. Cook, owner of the steamer, and "King of Egypt," as the natives called him; (3) the Sirdar of the Egyptian Army. I mention these objects of honor in the order which they were enumerated to me.

If Cook and his enterprise made an impression on Budge, it seems the reverse was also true, because the young Egyptologist was commissioned to prepare a work on ancient Egypt that was published by Cook & Son as *The Nile: Notes for Travellers in Egypt* in 1890 and given to every traveler that booked a Nile cruise; the book was updated and reprinted in a new edition no less than twelve times by 1912.

At around the same time the *Prince Abbas* and *Tewfik* were commissioned, John learned of a large river steamer under construction on the Rhône in France, which had been intended for the French government but, for whatever reason, was now surplus to requirements. John's right-hand man, Alexander Rostovitz, was sent over to take a look; he pronounced the boat fit for purpose and it was purchased. The French shipyard was also commissioned to build another steamer on precisely the same lines as the *Prince Abbas* and *Tewfik*. These two new French steamers were to be called, in the first case, *Rameses*, and the second, *Prince Mohammed Ali*, after Tewfik's second son. They were due to be completed and delivered by September 1886, but it wasn't until the first week of December that they finally left Marseilles towed behind larger, more powerful seagoing vessels for their journey across the Mediterranean. Not long out of port, severe gales battered the ships and they were forced to hug the coast, frequently beating a retreat to the safety of the nearest harbor; at one point one pair of vessels laying up at Naples and the other at Messina, waiting on more favorable weather. It was mid-January before the ships finally reached Alexandria. From here they were taken along the coast to Damietta and the mouth of the Nile, from where they could be towed up to Cairo.

As if the previous six weeks had not proved problematic enough, the *Rameses* proved too big to pass through the Nile Barrage, the system of locks, dams, and weirs just north of Cairo that regulated the flow of the river into the Delta. John sailed down from Cairo with sixty men and on assessing the problem ordered the boat's paddle wheels to be removed. The work involved cutting through thousands of rivets, a thankless task that occupied three days. Even then, the *Rameses* had to be forced through the lock. It was

A flag that meant business
In a March 1893 letter to his father, John, Frank Cook wrote that he had received a sketch of a proposed company flag from a Mr. Royle, but that he found it too elaborate and "flash." Frank proposed his own alternative design, which he argued should be as plain and businesslike as possible and definitely not red, "as nearly every flag on the river at the present time is of that colour"

Unlike the previous two boats built for Cook & Son's Nile fleet, the *Rameses* was constructed in France, on the Rhône. She was a considerably larger vessel, capable of carrying seventy passengers compared to the forty-four of the *Prince Abba*s and *Tewfik*

finally towed up to Cairo where 150 men, working in double shifts, had to put the boat back together again. In six days they replaced the crankshafts, paddles, and paddle boxes; they built large saloons and berths on the upper decks; they painted, decorated, and furnished. She, and the *Prince Mohammed Ali*, made their maiden runs to Aswan in January 1887, joining the other two new "first-class tourist steamers," the *Prince Abbas* and *Tewfik*, in being introduced during the 1886–87 season.

The amenities offered onboard the new steamers are described in Cook & Son's 1888 brochure: the boats are "constructed of the best possible materials; the hulls being steel plates throughout, the engines of the most approved description, and the passenger accommodation provided in accordance with our knowledge of the requirements of the travelling public, and in accordance with what we consider first class passengers are entitled to whilst travelling on the Nile."

No cabins contained more than two berths, and many just a single berth. First-class cabins were on the main and upper decks, second-class on the lower. All were fitted with electric bells to ring for service, and windows that featured a triple arrangement of glass, Venetian blinds, and wire gauze to keep out insects. The cabins shared bathrooms: ladies on the lower deck, men

above. Use of the bathrooms was now included in the fare, instead of being charged extra, as had been the case previously. Each steamer had a dining saloon on the forward upper deck and a private saloon for ladies. There was a piano, a small library, and "facilities for amusement" in the saloon, and the whole upper deck could be enclosed with canvas curtains at night.

All crew were now in the direct employ of Cook & Son, captains and engineers included. Each boat also carried a European doctor with a well-equipped medicine chest, although Cook & Son's literature pointedly highlighted that the professional services of these doctors were rarely required, and their presence onboard was chiefly as a comfort to travelers. A "first-class" chef oversaw the galley, and all the table appointments—glass, napery, china—were made especially for the steamers. There was (almost) everything that could make a voyage agreeable, reported the Reverend Charles Bell, who sailed aboard the *Rameses* in its second season on the Nile, "the only thing wanting to make the boat perfect is electric light, which might easily be supplied, and would add much to the comfort of the passengers."

Before the interruption of the Sudan campaigns, there had been a departure from Cairo every two weeks, but with the introduction of the new

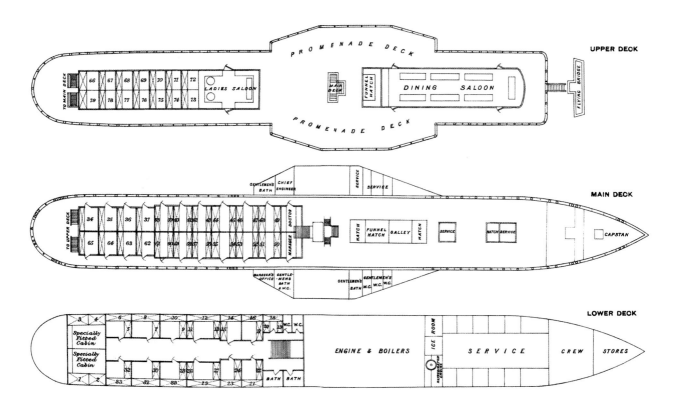

PREVIOUS SPREAD The *Rameses the Great* was the fifth boat to be built and added to Cook & Son's fleet in the space of just three years

ABOVE Although slightly smaller than the *Rameses* in terms of length, the *Rameses the Great* fitted more cabins on its three decks, with accommodation for up to seventy-nine passengers

fleet, departures were increased to a weekly service. Cook & Son was also able to resume sailings between the First and Second Cataracts. This was a voyage that formerly took fourteen days, scheduled as it was to connect with the Cairo–Aswan boats, but with the increased frequency of that service, the Second Cataract steamers now made the voyage from Shellal to Wadi Halfa and back in seven days. The route was operated by a newly purchased sternwheel steamer, the *Sethi*, which had cabins and berths for twenty-seven first-class passengers.

What was formerly the mail service between the railhead at Asyut and Aswan was also reinstated in 1887. Marketed as the "Cheap Express Service," it was initially operated by some of the old Egyptian government steamers, refitted and spruced up (the *Amosis*, *Pepi*, and *Thotmes*), but these proved inadequate to the task, and the following season they were replaced by three new, purpose-built steamers: the *Amenartas*, *Cleopatra*, and *Nefertari* (a fourth, the *Hatasoo*, was added in 1890). To prove their "express" credentials, in November 1888 John completed the run from Cairo to Aswan and back, a distance of 1,200 miles, in the *Cleopatra* in 122 hours, faster than anyone had ever done it before. With departures from Asyut at 5 a.m. each Tuesday and

Saturday, the Express was for travelers who wanted to spend less time and money on seeing the Nile. It only made short stops en route, including just a few hours at Qena and Edfu, but a whole day at Aswan. Luxor was a halt of only a few minutes but passengers could always get off, stay a few days at the Luxor Hotel, and catch the next Express. This gave the option of doing a Nile cruise in just fourteen or fifteen days, as opposed to twenty-one on the first-class steamers. It was less luxurious but also considerably less money.

The service still carried the mail, and in 1889 a new contract was made with the Egyptian government confirming Cook & Son as the official mail carrier to Middle and Upper Egypt, and conveyors of all military personnel and civil servants.

To be able to maintain his fleet, John purchased a large plot of riverside real estate at Bulaq, the riverside suburb of Cairo that had traditionally served as the city's port, and where Napoleon had established a boatyard back in 1799. This became Cook & Son's service depot, complete with dry docks, engineering sheds, and machine works. The yard's first major task was to assemble yet another new vessel. This was the *Rameses the Great*, which had been constructed at the Fairfield Works on the Clyde, after which it had been taken to pieces again and sent to Egypt in 3,750 cases. The railway trucks bringing the first portion of the ironwork arrived on 11 November 1889. John saw two posts, stem and stern, put in that day before leaving for Upper Egypt. On his return to Cairo, exactly a fortnight later, the reassembled hull was ready to be launched and on the fifteenth morning from the date of arrival of the first truck, *Rameses the Great* was put into the water. She was the largest steamer to date to be launched on the Nile and would remain so for the best part of the next twenty years. She did not carry many more passengers than the other boats in the fleet but her salons and deck space were more generous.

Again, the khedive was curious to see the new vessel, and once construction was finished he visited the steamer late one evening so he could receive a demonstration of the ship's 22,000-candle-power searchlight, which enabled it to sail at night. In January 1890, a distinguished company, including several ministers, the *sirdar* of the Egyptian army, and African explorer Henry Morton Stanley, assembled onboard the *Rameses the Great* for a trial cruise.

Since Thomas's retirement, John was now free to steer the company in what he believed was the more financially prudent course; this involved reversing his father's policy of travel for all and pushing in a more exclusive direction. Where Thomas had worked to make travel easier and cheaper,

All Cook & Son's new steamers had hulls, superstructure, engines, and boilers that were built in Britain or France, then disassembled to be put back together again at the company shipyard in Bulaq, where decks and cabins would be added

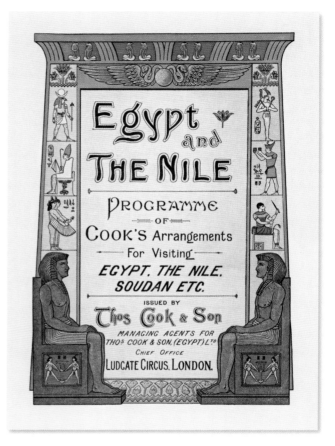

As the nineteenth century gave way to the twentieth, Cook's "Egypt and the Nile" brochures became thicker and thicker as the size of the fleet and services increased

John sought to make it more comfortable. In addition to the new first-class steamers he purchased a "very superior" steam launch, a small boat suitable for a party of not more than eight, which he called *Nitocris*, and which he advertised as a "steam *dahabiya*"—the vessel had no sails and so wasn't a *dahabiya* at all, but the word carried connotations of exclusivity that must have appealed to John. It provided, according to Cook's brochure, "the most luxurious mode of ascending the Nile" (this was the boat hired by the Conan Doyles in January 1896, see p. 80). A second private steam launch, the *Mena*, was added to the fleet in 1890. The company also developed its fleet of true *dahabiya*s, introducing the boats *Horus*, *Isis*, *Mansourah*, and *Osiris* for the season 1889–90; the *Ammon-Ra*, *Hathor*, and *Nepthis* for the following season; and the *Fostat*, *Gazelle*, *New Star*, and *Sultana* for the season after that. Revenues rose dramatically: in 1888 the two *dahabiya*s in the fleet earned the company £380; just five years later, now with thirteen *dahabiya*s, the earnings had leapt to £22,512.

Copy in the *Excursionist* boasted, "Having been patronized by the middle-class, we now count among our clientele the royal family and the highest aristocracy in the land." Certainly in Egypt the company had its fair share of distinguished clients, with Cook organizing exclusive charters around this time for the American millionaire Cornelius Vanderbilt and for the British consul-general in Egypt, Sir Evelyn Baring and party. In 1891, John also personally conducted the Egyptian head of state, Khedive Tewfik, from Asyut to the Second Cataract and back; that same year, Tewfik rewarded Cook & Son's investment in Egypt by conferring on John the Order of Commander of the Osmanieh. (When Tewfik died the following year a Cook's crew marched in the funeral procession.)

In just one season alone, 1895–96, the list of clients hiring Cook's *dahabiya*s (which now numbered twenty-eight) read like an edition of *Who's Who* and included the Earl of Gosford, Lord Compton, Prince Duleep Singh, Lord Farrer, the Earl of Jersey, the Earl of Powis, Lord Wantage, the Duke of Marlboro, Lord Ashburton, and H.I.H. Archduke Ferdinand.

Meanwhile, the company was heavily promoting its Egyptian investment over in Europe and America. For the 1889 World's Fair in Paris, held in the shadow of Messr. Eiffel's not-quite-complete tower, Cook & Son had a pavilion on the "Rue du Caire," at which it displayed a large-scale model of the Temple of Horus at Edfu, as well as detailed and impressive models of its new steamers, the *Prince Abbas*, *Rameses*, *Rameses the Great*, a couple of *dahabiya*s, and a sectional model of the *Hatasoo*. Four years later, they were all on show again on the "Street in Cairo" at the 1893 Chicago World's Fair, where they competed for the public's attention with performances by the sensation known as Little Egypt, the woman who introduced the hoochee-coochee, or bellydance, to America (actually the Syrian wife of a Greek-Chicagoan restaurant owner).

In the last decade of the twentieth century, a trip to Egypt was widely seen as one of the most exciting winter activities available to the rich. In February 1891, the visit to Egypt of the *Augusta Victoria*, the Hamburg America Line's latest, luxury, ocean-going vessel, making what is considered the world's first pleasure cruise, meant that Cairo's hotels were so overcrowded that Cook & Son could take advantage by deploying three of its steamers as floating hotels to relieve the pressure. Not that the company had much in the way of spare berths: passenger numbers for each successive season surpassed those that had gone before. During the season of 1891–92 there was such a spike that John took the decision to add yet another steamer. This new vessel was again built on the Clyde, where it was taken apart and then shipped over to

Cook's presence at the 1893 World's Fair in Chicago heavily showcased the company's new Nile fleet

be reassembled in Egypt. The *Rameses the Third* was launched into regular service on 17 January 1893—but only after the by now customary visit from the khedive, now His Highness Abbas Hilmi, successor to Tewfik.

At a speech to mark the launch, John recalled that when he had made his first trip to the Nile twenty-three years before, there had been only one passenger-carrying steamer and 136 *dahabiya*s; now there were fifteen steamers, all running under his ownership, and not more than thirty *dahabiya*s. Amelia Edwards, who had died the previous year, would not have been happy.

Since 1885, John had been spending every winter in Egypt: partly because he found the warm climate agreeable to his health and partly because he had fallen in love with the Nile, but mainly because by the time *Rameses the Third* came into service, half of Thomas Cook & Son's entire global revenue came from its Nile steamer service.

Aiding John in running the Egyptian business was his youngest son, Bert, who had accompanied him up the Nile to Dongola in 1884. Bert was manager of Nile operations, although judging by correspondence in the Thomas Cook archive, he struggled to live up to his father's exacting standards. John's frequent letters contain litanies of complaints, sometimes filling more than a dozen pages: there are not enough saddles being carried onboard ("I want to know who is to blame for such neglect"); the boats have the wrong kind of soap ("On the *Rameses* I see Yardley's Windsor Soap instead of Franks soap—how is this?"); the games carried aboard the steamers

And still the fleet kept growing, with the introduction in 1893 of yet another boat named for one of ancient Egypt's mightiest pharaohs, *Rameses the Third*

The company of Cook & Son enjoyed a close relationship with the rulers of Egypt; here Thomas Albert "Bert" Cook (in the bowler hat) has his portrait taken alongside H.H. Abbas Hilmi and H.H. Prince Mohammed Ali on the occasion of a royal visit to England in 1886

for passengers' amusement are incomplete ("One of the bezique boxes on the boat has no counters, showing some mean skunk has stolen them"); the plumbing is poor and the WCs don't work ("It appears to me that the boat has been sent away without anybody making the slightest inspection"); below-decks crew are seen on the upper, tourist decks ("With all deference to these gentlemen they are not yet as cleanly as they should be"). "I begin to wonder whether we shall ever have business run properly from the Cairo office," he writes in exasperation. However, John never directly accuses Bert of negligence, always pointing the finger at someone else. One suspects that Bert, the youngest of three sons, was John's favorite.

George Steevens, who sailed on the *Rameses the Great* as far as Aswan and then on the *Prince Abbas* up to the Second Cataract, paid tribute to the company's dominance in his book *Egypt in 1898*:

> The nominal suzerain of Egypt is the Sultan; its real suzerain is Lord Cromer [Consul-General Sir Evelyn Baring]. Its nominal Governor is the Khedive; its real Governor, for a final touch of comic opera, is Thomas Cook & Son. Cook's representative is the first person you meet in Egypt, and you go on meeting him. He sees you in; he sees you through; he sees you out. You see the back of a native—turban, long blue gown, red girdle, bare brown legs; "How truly Oriental!" you say. Then he turns round, and you see "Cook's Porter" emblazoned across his breast. "You travel Cook, sir," he grins; "All

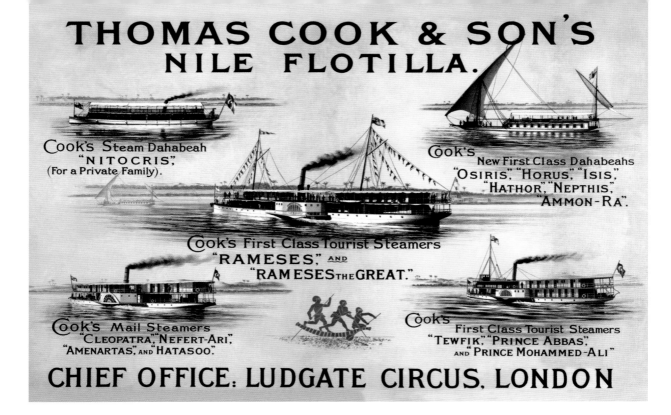

THOMAS COOK & SON'S
NILE FLOTILLA.

Cook's Steam Dahabeah "NITOCRIS", (For a Private Family).

Cook's New First Class Dahabeahs "OSIRIS", "HORUS", "ISIS", "HATHOR", "NEPHTIS", "AMMON-RA".

Cook's First Class Tourist Steamers "RAMESES", AND "RAMESES THE GREAT."

Cook's Mail Steamers "CLEOPATRA", "NEFERT-ARI", "AMENARTAS", AND "HATASOO".

Cook's First Class Tourist Steamers "TEWFIK", "PRINCE ABBAS", AND "PRINCE MOHAMMED-ALI"

CHIEF OFFICE: LUDGATE CIRCUS, LONDON

A poster advertising Cook and Son's fine new Nile flotilla. It must have been produced around 1889, the year that *Rameses the Great* was added to the fleet, possibly for that year's World's Fair in Paris

right." And it is all right: Cook carries you, like a nursing father, from one end of Egypt to the other.

In a tale that smacks of the apocryphal, Steevens describes how Lord Cromer went up the Nile with John Cook, and they went to visit a desert sheikh near Luxor. The sheikh was unaware that since 1882 the British were in control of Egypt.

"Haven't you ever heard of me?" asked Lord Cromer. The sheikh said he hadn't.

"Have you heard of Mr. Cook?"

"Everybody knows Cook Pasha," he replied.

The American magazine *Blackwood's*, in its August 1899 issue, put it more bluntly: "Cook simply owns Egypt."

There was at least one occasion on which John Mason Cook met his match. In 1896 the British government embarked on a new campaign to reconquer Sudan. Cook & Son was not so intimately involved this time around, and the company was only requested to move men and supplies up to Aswan. Beyond this point, the leader of the expeditionary force, Lord Horatio Kitchener, had assembled his own fleet of gunboats and was constructing a railway across the desert to transport his army. Cook's main tourist operations were not interrupted, except that Kitchener forbade its steamers to sail between the First and Second Cataracts because he did not want tourists impeding the war effort. In typically bullish fashion, John instructed his boats to proceed anyway; the equally hardheaded Kitchener countered by running a telegraph wire across the river at Shellal to stop any boats going south. If Cook's agents disobeyed his orders, he decreed, then they would be tried in a military court. John had no choice but to back down.*

It may be that with Nubian operations on hold for the moment John's thoughts turned to upgrading options in Aswan, so tourists who might otherwise have taken a cruise to the Second Cataract might be persuaded to spend more time in the Nile-side town. Since 1877, Cook's agent in Upper Egypt, Ferdinand Pagnon, had been operating the Luxor Hotel, which, due to demand, had been expanded several times. By 1890, it had beds for 120, plus amenities that ran to a billiard room, tennis courts, luscious gardens, and an adjacent farm supplying vegetables, poultry, meat, and milk, not just for the hotel's table but also for the company's steamers. Cook & Son had also bought a second property, the Karnak Hotel, which provided an additional fifty rooms. At Aswan, for several seasons starting with 1892–93, John had moored the steamer *Sethi* to serve as a floating hotel. In 1894, Pagnon acquired the Hotel Assouan but this was of modest size and so, not long after, John purchased a large plot of cliff-top land overlooking the First Cataract. Here, Cook & Son built a wholly new and grand hotel, which opened in 1900 as the Cataract. Initially it was leased to Pagnon, but in 1904 it was sold to the Upper Egypt Hotels Co., a consortium headed up by Charles Baehler, owner of Shepheard's in Cairo, but in which Cook & Son also had a stake.

Three years later, the Upper Egypt Hotels Co. expanded its portfolio with the inauguration of the regal Winter Palace at Luxor, welcomed by the local press as "the finest and most elaborately schemed hotel within the land of Egypt." With a Nile fleet of luxurious, modern vessels and interests in two luxurious, modern Upper Egyptian hotels, Cook & Son could boast with forgivable hyperbole that "On no other river can a voyage be taken with so much luxury as is possible on this classic river under our arrangements."

Hieroglyphs in tribute to "John son of the Sun Cook," "king of Upper and Lower Egypt," the "Lord of the Nile" who "gives bread into the mouths of the people of Thebes," reputedly "discovered" at Aswan but possibly concocted by a keen Cook & Son employee

---

* A twenty-two-year-old Winston Churchill took part in the campaign: "Here we are on the Nile," he wrote. "The railway is left, and progress is by steamer. One was already waiting. The versatile and ubiquitous Cook has undertaken the arrangements, as his name painted on everything clearly showed."

LIFE ABOARD

"I wonder that there are not people who spend their lives on Cook's Nile steamers, just as they spend their lives at golf-clubs which have bed-rooms." DOUGLAS SLADEN, 1908

❝ This morning we started for the Nile steamer, with our small trunks only. As we drove across the bridge to the wharf just beyond, the little double-decker floating on the water looked clean and fresh, a most inviting home for a three weeks' excursion. The manager of the steamship company was at the boat to see us off, and presented each passenger with a permit for which the ordinary tourist pays a pound, and which secures the entree to all the monuments of Egypt. He also gave to each a copy of Dr. Wallis Budge's book on Egypt.

There are only about thirty passengers, for the season has barely begun, this being but the second trip of the *Rameses* up the Nile. As we put off from shore the barefoot Egyptian sailors with long poles pushed us clear of the wharf, singing in unison as they worked.

The author is Blanche Mabury Carson, a forty-year-old widow who, in December 1904, had recently arrived in Egypt from New York, via the SS *Finland* of the transatlantic Red Star Line. She and her companion, the enigmatic B., were well traveled in Europe, where they had been a bit sniffy

OPPOSITE Aboard the *Serapis*, a small steamer built in 1900, with just ten cabins accommodating fifteen passengers

LEFT And more passengers arriving to take their cabins on an unidentifiable steamer at Cairo

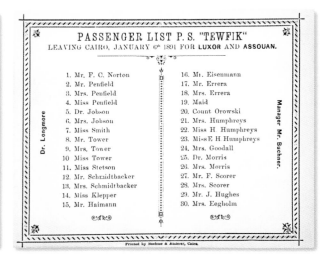

Cook's Nile Service

P. S. "Tewfik"

Cook's Nile Service

P. S. "Tewfik"

PASSENGER LIST P. S. "TEWFIK"
LEAVING CAIRO, JANUARY 6ᵗʰ 1891 FOR LUXOR AND ASSOUAN.

1. Mr. F. C. Norton	16. Mr. Eisenmann
2. Mr. Penfield	17. Mr. Errera
3. Mrs. Penfield	18. Mrs. Errera
4. Miss Penfield	19. Maid
5. Dr. Jobson	20. Count Orowski
6. Mrs. Jobson	21. Mrs. Humphreys
7. Miss Smith	22. Miss H Humphreys
8. Mr. Tower	23. Miss E H Humphreys
9. Mrs. Tower	24. Mrs. Goodall
10 Miss Tower	25. Dr. Morris
11. Miss Stetson	26. Mrs. Morris
12. Mr. Schmidtbacker	27. Mr. F. Scorer
13. Mrs. Schmidtbacker	28. Mrs. Scorer
14. Miss Klepper	29. Mr. J. Hughes
15. Mr. Haimann	30. Mrs. Eegholm

Dr. Longmore

Manager Mr. Buchner.

Printed by Boehme & Anderer, Cairo.

ABOVE Through the 1890s, and possibly later, Cook & Son's distributed beautifully decorated passenger lists with the names of all sailing aboard, although, in the case here, it was not necessary to identify hired help by name

OPPOSITE The passengers gather on deck to make each other's acquaintance

about the "Cookies" they encountered, but Egypt, and their onward destination of India, were outside of the ladies' comfort zone (as Carson put it, "so remote and so barbaric"), so they had opted for the protection of a conducted party.

They joined the boat at Cook's moorings just south of the Qasr al-Nil Bridge in central Cairo. These were on the east bank, and the ladies had to cross the bridge because they were arriving from the Mena House, the grand hotel beside the Pyramids, which lay on the west bank.

They would have been reassured by what they found onboard. Cook's boats were equal to the best hotels. There was the same procession of Arab porters in gowns waiting to seize newcomers' luggage, overseen by a European manager, or purser, who would possibly have been Italian, as many were. The cabins were spacious, with good beds, not bunks, high enough from the ground to take two or three ladies' dress-baskets underneath—an important consideration, given that people changed their clothes often in the smart society of Cook's boats.

The steamers would usually depart at 10 a.m., and passengers would barely have time to unpack and settle into their cabins before the first scheduled stop, which came just a couple of hours later, around midday. This was Badrashin, landing point for an excursion across the fields by donkey to the ancient capital of Memphis and its burial grounds at Saqqara, which included the Pyramid of Unas, recently cleared out and opened at the expense of Thomas Cook & Son.

All were back aboard in time for five o'clock tea, served on the upper deck in the open salon, amidships. This was furnished with easy chairs, tables, Oriental carpets, and potted plants, and was a cozy and comfortable place for lounging, writing letters, playing chess, and consulting guidebooks and volumes from the ship's library. As the light dwindled and darkness came on, the crew

Our artist writes: " The social process of 'breaking the ice' is in a Nile steamer as in all steamers, only more so. As the tonnage of the boat does not run into five figures, opportunities are frequent. Then, for the entire trip everyone is of one mind, bound for the same tombs and temples, dam and cataract. Altogether there should not be much effort required."

DRAWN BY REGINALD CLEAVER

Time onboard was spent resting, writing letters, promenading the deck, and watching the scenery go by. "We have had a perfect panorama of palms all day," wrote Blanche Maybury Carson, voyaging on the *Rameses* in 1904. "You mustn't get tired of hearing about palms, for they're all there is in the shape of trees"

would let down canvas awnings on both sides of the deck and the electric lights were turned on, "making it as warm and bright as a lady's drawing-room," thought Mrs. Carson.

There would be a couple more hours' sailing after Badrashin, before the captain halted the boat for the night at Ayat. The tourist steamers did not sail at night because it was impossible to navigate the river's channels and dodge the sandbanks in the dark.

On the second day of the standard twenty-one-day cruise there were no stops. Passengers rested and eased themselves into the languorous routine of the river. After breakfast they could watch the scenery idle by, the palm groves, sugarcane fields, and the occasional tall chimneys of sugar factories that possibly injected an unwelcome note of modernism in the otherwise timeless landscape.

They could also inspect their fellow voyagers; after all, they would be spending a lot of time in each other's company over the next three weeks. Trips up the Nile were still not cheap and the steamers continued to largely be the preserve of the better off. Heading toward the end of the nineteenth century, a goal of the savvy traveler abroad was to shun the well-worn tourist haunts, such as Italy and the Rhine. Those who could afford it increasingly went farther afield or holidayed out of season—a Nile cruise achieved both.

On day three, they sailed by Gebel al-Deir, the hill topped by a Coptic monastery; this was where the priests swam out naked to Miss Riggs's boat back in 1869, but at Cook's request the patriarch in Cairo had put a stop to that and now they rowed out fully clothed to beg for their baksheesh. That afternoon, the boats would call briefly at Minya before continuing on to Beni Hasan, where they would lay up for the night. Early the next morning there would be an expedition up to the high terrace of rock-cut tombs for which the place was famous. As at all riverside halts, passengers going ashore would be greeted by an unruly mob of donkey boys; the donkey boys at Beni Hasan were considered to be the unruliest of the lot. They would continually thwack their animals on the behind, making them leap forward and gallop, because the boys were impatient to get back to the boat and receive their fee. Mrs. Carson mastered the art of staying in the saddle but not everyone was so capable:

> Miss Martha, though eager to make the excursion, had been timid and doubtful of her ability to sit so small an animal. We had over-persuaded her, however, and after several attempts, for one hundred and eighty pounds is no light matter to be hoisted into a saddle, Hafiz managed to mount the lady. She had stipulated for two donkey boys, and was assigned a couple of tall youths who ran along and propped her up on each side. The necessity of jumping so much *avoirdupois* into the saddle caused our dragoman thereafter to discourage our heavy-weights from going on further excursions.
>
> On the home stretch Miss Martha was the last in. As I looked back I saw her coming, her bonnet on the back of her head. Her face, burned red by the heat of the sun, bore a look of exquisite anguish as she gripped her two Arabs tightly about the neck. The weary donkey ambled gently forward. The runners nearly exhausted by strangulation, and anxious to end their agony as soon as possible, kept whacking the animal, allowing no pauses despite the outcries of its rider.

There were advantages to being first back to the boat: the lead rider escaped the dust of the twenty riders behind, and they were first into a hot bath back onboard. However, anyone who hadn't bathed on a Nile steamer before was in for a surprise. Although the bath and bathroom were clinically white, the water out of the taps was Nile water, which tended to look like liquid chocolate. One voyager did wonder after bathing in the "fertilizing mud" what crops might grow on his body—"small plantations of sugar-cane, with here and there, perhaps, a stray mushroom." The Baedeker guide to Egypt also reminded gentlemen that steamers sometimes ran jarringly aground, which was something to bear in mind when shaving.

From Beni Hasan, the steamer sailed on another twenty miles upriver to moor at the town of Asyut. Early next morning, a crew member would go ashore to collect the daily papers and any post that had been sent up from

A fellow passenger of Mrs. Carson's required two boys to prop her up when making excursions by donkey

ABOVE AND OPPOSITE The salon on the promenade deck was the focal point of boat life. This is where everyone gathered after dinner, in a lounge space furnished with a library for the bookish and a piano for the gregarious

Cairo. Passengers would find their letters on a plate when they sat down to breakfast—return letters could be placed in a letterbox onboard, which was emptied last thing at night. At Asyut the mail was carried to and from Cairo by train, but farther upriver it went on the Express Service steamers, which raced up and down the river in far less time than the dawdling passenger steamers.

The first part of that day was spent in the bazaar, although local traders did their best to render the excursion unnecessary by spreading their wares on the riverbank, including gold and silver bangles, and Coptic veils of cotton and silk threaded with more gold and silver. Departure would be at noon, with no further stops until the boat moored for the night at Tahta.

There would be no stops the following day, either. As George Steevens, passenger on the *Rameses the Great* in 1898, saw it, there was "just enough excursioning ashore to persuade you that you are not lazy, and just enough lazing aboard to assure you that you are enjoying the rest." The now forgotten, but in his time prolific, English travel writer Douglas Sladen was a passenger on the same boat in 1907. "On the days when there are no excursions," he wrote, "the particular young man sometimes breaks out into silk suits and wonderful socks, or, at any rate, rare and irreproachable flannels, just as the girl who has come to conquer Cairo society rings the gamut of summer extravagances. They have the moral courage for at least two different costumes between breakfast and dinner."

There was also an American millionaire on Sladen's boat whose appearance at breakfast served as a barometer for the day ahead.

If he had on a suit of eau-de-Nil-coloured Shantung silk, with a ribbon to match round his panama, and patent-kid shoes, we knew that we were going to be all day on board taking meals and Kodaks. If he was in immaculate white flannels with snow-white boots of a kind of doeskin and a white felt Monte Carlo hat we knew that we were only going to do little jaunts, such as walking off the steamer to a temple, which a considerate Pharaoh had pinned to the bank. But if he was in any of his adorable pale dove or biscuit riding-suits, and hung a helmet on the hat-rack, we knew that we had a long donkey ride before us.

Sladen would start the day onboard with a cup of tea at sunrise, which he would drink in bed while watching the banks of the Nile warm up outside his window. Before most others were awake, he'd have a bath, unless the boat was passing something of particular interest, in which case he'd put an overcoat over his pajamas and go and sit in the sun gallery, which was at the front of the promenade deck and glazed all around. This, he wrote, would always dismay the crew, who hated passengers seeing the deck before they had swept it with their ostrich-feather brooms.

He enjoyed his breakfasts, which he described as being like country-house meals, starting with porridge, and proceeding with bacon and eggs; fish and other hot dishes; ham, tongue, chicken, and other cold fare; and ending with jam and marmalade. Afterwards, he would join other passengers back in the sun gallery, to see whatever there was to see. Since the whole of habitable Egypt clings to the Nile, there was always plenty

Labels were pasted onto the luggage of new arrivals to make sure pieces found their way to the correct cabin

going on, from women washing pots or clothes, to children leading animals down to drink. All writers mentioned the buffalo-propelled *saqya*s (waterwheels) and *shaduf*s (a pole-and-bucket device to raise water), used by villagers to irrigate their fields.

Other than the domesticated buffalo, there was little in the way of wildlife to be seen, mostly just birds, though these were in abundance, including, but not limited to, Griffon and Egyptian vultures, imperial eagles and spotted eagles, kestrels, lesser kestrels, peregrines and other falcons, Egyptian eagle owls, ibises, ducks, Egyptian geese, various kingfishers, herons, storks and cranes, spoonbills, plovers, grey-headed yellow and whitewinged wagtails, desert bullfinch, quail, Egyptian swifts, bee-eaters, pigeons, and turtledoves. Although Cook & Son had a policy of no shooting from their steamers, this didn't preclude parties going ashore with their guns. Helen Mary Tirard, who was sailing aboard the *Rameses* in February 1890, records that three young men from her boat went inland and shot twenty-two pigeons, an owl, a hoopoe, and an unidentified "pretty green bird with orange wings."

Mrs. Carson looked in vain for crocodiles. She'd seen little boys on the streets of Cairo carrying stuffed crocodiles on their heads, leading her to think she might see one sunning itself on the sandbanks, but by this time it was about forty years since the last one was spotted north of the First Cataract.

There was also the river traffic, particularly the various sailboats, laden with cane, cotton, or grain, which Mrs. Carson thought with their crossed lateen sails resembled swallows resting on the water. Nothing more picturesque, she wrote, can be imagined than a fleet of these gliding by.

There were the other steamers, too: those on the return leg heading back downriver to Cairo, the Express Service steamers. There was a strict protocol for engagement laid out in the company's Instructions to Managers, which involved the use of signal flags: a blue flag meant "Make to shore or drop anchor midstream for important communication"; green, "Go easy or stop midstream and wait for our felucca"; yellow, "Mail for you left at Asyut"; white, "Mail for you left at Luxor"; blue and green, "Mail for you left at Aswan"; yellow and white, "Can you spare fresh provisions? If so, give one long whistle, and wait for our felucca"; blue and white, "We have provisions for you; send your felucca"; and so on.

There were also various government steamers, including one at the disposal of the head of the Antiquities Service, and steamers belonging to rival companies, more on which later. Under no circumstances, however, were Cook's steamers to salute a steamer of a competing company unless it saluted first, then the salute had to be returned but only out of respect for the Egyptian flag.

OPPOSITE AND ABOVE The larger boats, the first-class steamers on the Cairo–Aswan service, carried upwards of forty staff onboard. The crew who ran the boat answered to the Egyptian captain, while those who attended the passengers were directed by the European boat manager

While the passengers sat and observed, the crew in white robes, red tarbooshes, crimson sashes, and slippers hovered round with teapots, milk jugs, and sugar basins, and a dozen different kinds of Huntley & Palmers biscuits. On days with no excursions it was left to nature to provide the day's focal point, which came each evening with sunset; then, as now, sunsets on the Nile were blazing affairs of orange, red, and purple, spectacular enough to draw even the most indolent on deck.

Soon afterward it would be time for a suitably lavish dinner, after which the itinerary for the following day would be announced, a task undertaken by the senior of the two onboard dragomans. The steamers were captained by the *rais*, who actually sailed the vessel, and who was second in authority only to the ship's European manager, but the character who most determined the experience of the passengers was the dragoman. He was the tour guide, translator, decipherer of hieroglyphs, donkey-boy beater, proxy haggler, and all-round general fixer. For the tourist he was the main interface with Egypt.

Douglas Sladen considered himself lucky that he had Muhammad, the doyen of Cook's, for his chief dragoman. "He is a dragoman of the old school, who knows his subject well, but is even more endeared to the tourist by the picturesqueness of himself and the thirty changes of raiment, which he takes on board the ship with him." Blanche Mabury Carson's dragoman was the splendidly named Claudius Hafiz, who had once accompanied the "richest man in America," Cornelius Vanderbilt, up the Nile, and who would make his entrance into the dining saloon each evening during dessert. He would deliver a description of the sights to be seen on the following day, with all the

ABOVE Cook's Nile Service Turkish-style coffee cup

RIGHT As dinner comes to an end, the boat's dragoman outlines the following day's itinerary

Menu

"EGYPT."

Cairo, 7th December 1907

DEJEUNER.

Niersteiner	Hors d'Oeuvres Moscouvite
	Filets de Soles Chezsol
	Timballe de Raviolis Piemontaise
	Chapons à la Doria
	Céléris à la Moélle
Pommery & Greno Nature 1900	Haricots verts au beurre
	Chateaubriands Mirabeau
Perrier & Jouet Extra-Dry	Salade Jardinière
	Salade de Saison
	Apple Pie
	Gâteau Millefeuilles
	Glace Arlequin
	Gâteau "Egypt"
Liqueurs	Stilton
	Fruits
	Café Turque

facts and history delivered from memory, and also including a reminder of the importance of taking along their monuments pass:

The little red tickette,
O do not forget it!
For if you don't take it,
You can't pass the wickette!

He concluded every evening's presentation with the same injunction: "No donkey-racing allowed!"

After a full day's sailing, the passengers would be eager for distraction, which would be provided early on the morning of the seventh day with the arrival at Qena. On shore, the donkeys would be saddled for an excursion to the celebrated site of Dendara, and the tourists' first encounter with the overwhelming scale, intricacies, and beauty of an ancient Egyptian temple. Once all were back onboard, the steamer would continue south, and it would be a relatively short sail before visible ahead off to the left, protruding above the palms, would be the slender obelisks and solidly geometric pylons of Karnak.

Douglas Sladen noted that the boat's voyage south was accompanied by an evolution in the attitude of his fellow passengers: "Early on the trip they cannot all be persuaded to take the excursions. When they have seen Dendara, the voyagers of Cook are as changed as a hooligan who has heard the call of the Salvation Army. And lo and behold, on the evening of the day on which they have been appetized at Dendara, they are at Luxor, which is the happy hunting-ground of the Kingdom of Cook."

ABOVE LEFT Cook's Nile Service branded glasses

ABOVE Judging by this lunch menu (steak, fish, ravioli, various vegetable dishes, salads, three types of cake and pastry, ice cream, cheese, and fruit), the cuisine aboard Cook's steamers was polished and plentiful

ABOVE AND OPPOSITE The ideal dragoman, according to Douglas Sladen, has a fund of good stories, which he tells with unconsciously theatrical gestures; a great deal of authority when dealing with donkey boys and curio sellers; wonderful tact and patience with the exacting or stupid people whom he has to show over ruins; and unfailing wit and cheerfulness

Having traveled 460 miles, the boat had reached Luxor; here, in the shadow of the riverside Temple of Luxor, it would tie up and reprovision, while its passengers spent three days following their dragoman from temple to tomb. On clear moonlit nights, the sightseeing would begin almost immediately with a nighttime donkey ride to Karnak; if the moon was insufficiently luminous, the magic would wait until morning.

If Dendara was an appetizer, Karnak was the visitors' first great banquet of antiquity, three temples each with a vast enclosure incorporating chapels, halls, and dozens of smaller temples. Blanche Mabury Carson found the centerpiece Great Hall, which Charles Edwin Wilbour described as "a Yosemite forest in stone," more of a building site, as under the direction of French Egyptologist Georges Legrain, teams of workers were laboring to reconstruct eleven columns that had tumbled down during an earthquake in 1899. The huge stone drums that make up the columns were being piled one on top of another, using mounded earth to form a slope up which the upper drums were rolled using ropes, much as they must have been in the original construction of the temple. It would be possible to spend a week at Karnak and not see everything, but there was lunch to be had back onboard, followed by the Temple of Luxor afterward, and a visit to the bazaar before dinner.

The next morning, the tourists would be ferried in small boats across to the west bank where, as Sladen describes it, "the donkey-boys are gesticulating on the shore like golf caddies on a Sunday morning, while their donkeys are behaving like boys in church." There is, he continues, "no place like Thebes for a donkey-ride. It is full of nice sandy tracks for a gallop, and the Colossi and temples"—which on this second day at Luxor included Medinet Habu, Deir al-Medina, and the Ramesseum—"are a nice distance apart from each other. There are curio stalls outside every temple, where you can buy mummy hawks for fivepence, and cats for a trifle more."

On Sladen's trip the afternoon was spent attending camel, buffalo, and donkey races held behind the Winter Palace in aid of Cook's Luxor Hospital. Visitors were encouraged to enter the donkey races but, said Sladen, the residents always win them because they have their own donkeys, trained to do as they're told—notably trotting in a straight line.

On the third day, the tourists were again ferried over to the West Bank and saddled up for the long donkey ride to Deir al-Bahari and the Temple of Queen Hatshepsut, followed by refreshments at Cook's own, purpose-built rest house, the "Chalet Hatasoo." Rejuvenated, everybody would then remount and set off along the base of the cliffs, around into the Valley of the Kings for an afternoon chasing long-dead kings down deep into their rock-cut tombs.

The Chalet Hatasoo, the rest house that Cook & Son had built beside the Temple of Hatshepsut to provide shade and refreshment

Examining the itinerary a Cook's tourist followed a century or more ago might give the impression that the experience was quite similar to today's. Not so. The work of discovering and recording the pharaonic sites had only recently begun, and this was still very much a country of discovery. Ancient Egypt was still being unearthed—quite literally. From the deck of the moored *Rameses* in 1890, Helen Mary Tirard was witness to an army of laborers digging out Luxor Temple, with five hundred children carrying away baskets of dirt that they tipped into the Nile. In the brief time she was there, she saw a frieze of chariots gradually emerge as part of an outer wall was cleared. Visitors to the Pyramid of Hawara, to which Egyptologist Flinders Petrie had succeeded in opening up access in 1888, had to strip down in its upper chamber, then squeeze through a small hole in the roof to drop down into a chamber that was waist deep in water. Other passages could only be explored by crawling nearly flat in the soft mud that filled them.

Government-backed authority had yet to successfully regulate the approach to archaeology and its finds, and there was almost a Gold Rush feel about Upper Egypt, with a single officer from the Antiquities Service acting as a lone, beleaguered sheriff.

Luxor was well known as a place to procure antiquities, though buyers had to beware the thriving trade in forged items. So well made were many of these things that only the practiced eye of a connoisseur could tell the difference. Several of the consuls in Luxor kept stashes of genuine antiquities for sale to foreign visitors: Helen Mary Tirard bought silver bracelets from the German consul, while, two years earlier, the Reverend Charles Bell was invited by the

Tourists receive some pointed elucidation from their dragoman

English consul to the unraveling of a mummy in a hunt for the scarabs and pieces of jewelry that were sometimes bound in the wrappings. It was an illegal trade but these officials were able to take advantage of the diplomatic immunity that kept them exempt from the occasional raids by the Antiquities Service on local dealers and shops.

On her last afternoon in Luxor, Mrs. Carson paid a visit to a Cook's steamer that had just gotten in from Aswan and was anchored near by, and browsed the local curio and antiquities shops. Everyone, she reports, bought enameled lotus hatpins and brooches of real green beetles. A bridal couple from Chicago, fellow passengers, were taken by a green-stone cartouche that the dealer said came from the mummy of Ramesses and cost eight dollars; when asked if he had any more like it he pulled twenty-two from a drawer and the pair bought the lot.

Helen Mary Tirard noted that some members of her party found other forms of amusement: one evening most of the men went to see a performance by Egypt's infamous *ghawazi* dancers. She says they came back "disgusted with the whole performance, which seems quite devoid of grace or modesty," but then, they would tell the ladies that, wouldn't they?

After three busy days, the steamers departed Luxor, eleven days in total since leaving Cairo. The next stop was reached after just four hours of sailing. At Esna, passengers would go ashore to visit the town's largely buried Temple of Khnum, where a lofty central hall was the only part excavated. Within an hour they would be back onboard and the boat would steam on to tie up for the night at Edfu, where the next morning after breakfast they would tour the Ptolemaic-era Temple of Horus.

From Edfu, the steamers pushed on, past the limestone cliffs of Gebel Silsila, where the ancient Egyptians quarried sandstone blocks cut for the temples of Upper Egypt. If time permitted, passengers were put ashore to visit, but the main aim that day was to get to Kom Ombo in daylight. Dramatically perched on a rock plateau overlooking the river, Kom Ombo's twin temples were dedicated jointly to the falcon-headed god Horus and the crocodile-headed god Sobek, and this is where Mrs. Carson did finally get to see her crocodiles, albeit in mummified form.

On the thirteenth morning the steamers departed Kom Ombo, and it was just a few hours' sail before easing in to the moorings at Aswan, 595 miles distant from Cairo, and the farthest south the regular services sailed.

At the northern end of the First Cataract, Aswan was a natural halting place where, on a plain on the river's eastern shore, traders from the north and south had met for centuries—the town's name is derived from the ancient Egyptian

A Cook & Son's ticket for passage from Girga to Aswan and back to Cairo, issued November 1893 and personally authorized by Frank Henry Cook

PREVIOUS SPREAD Tourists at the Ramesseum on the West Bank at Luxor. "There is no place like Thebes for a donkey-ride," wrote Douglas Sladen: "It is full of nice sandy tracks for a gallop, and the Colossi and temples are a nice distance apart from each other"

ABOVE Passengers enjoying some winter sun aboard the Cook & Son steamer *Rameses*, some time in the 1890s

for 'marketplace.' The bazaar was (and still is) one of Aswan's major attractions. On the first afternoon the steamer passengers were left to explore on their own. The Nile is particularly beautiful here and many chose to hire a felucca and flit between the islands that dot the river, typically putting shore on Elephantine Island, site of an ancient Nilometer, temple ruins, and native villages set in among the palm groves.

Sightseeing on the next day was more structured. After an early breakfast, passengers were saddled up on donkeys and led out on the desert road, where an hour's ride would bring them to Shellal. Here they would exchange the donkeys for a place in a small boat that would carry them over to the island of Philae, to picnic among the ruins Egypt.

Returning from Philae, instead of heading back to the landing, the boats would drift downriver to deposit tourists on the bank just above the First Cataract, at a spot where there was a striking view of the churning waters. There the donkeys would be waiting to carry them back to Aswan. Alternatively, if there were any passengers wishing to 'shoot' the cataract, Cook's agent could organize it—at the passengers' own expense, and risk.

Any passengers booked to continue on to the Second Cataract would now transfer to a smaller steamer, waiting at Shellal, for the one-week return voyage to Wadi Halfa and back. This was not part of Blanche Mabury Carson's plans; instead, after a two-day stay in Aswan, she was back aboard the *Rameses* and sleeping as early in the morning the boat eased out into the river and allowed the current to propel it back north. She did not remain sleeping for long: "Just after leaving Aswan at five this morning, we were awakened by a great shouting and splashing. The ship had run aground."

While it had taken two weeks to come up the river, with the tide in the boat's favor, it could steam back to Cairo in a week. The landscape would now flash by much faster, "like a moving panorama," thought Mrs. Carson, only it was she who was doing the speeding. There was a further day at Luxor and a day at Abydos visiting the Temple of Seti. The final stop was a half-day at Asyut, where anybody in a hurry could catch a train that would have them back in Cairo that same evening. Those who remained could enjoy a further two days of water-borne indolence.

"For three weeks we have been privileged spectators of these homely scenes and time-honoured customs perpetuated through centuries," wrote Mrs. Carson, in the final paragraph of *From Cairo to the Cataract.*

Members of the serving staff of the first-class passenger steamer *Rameses*

> Their familiarity makes them only the more fascinating. Although it is but three, tea is being served on deck, a last courtesy from the ship. Already the domes and minarets of the Citadel are in sight, while the grim Pyramids have been hovering in the western distance for some hours past. The river is crowded with blue-bordered sails all bound for Cairo. As we bear down upon fleet after fleet, they part and let us pass. The palaces and gardens of the eastern bank now fly by, and at last we come to anchor, just this side of the great Nile bridge.

One last thing remained, and that was for the passengers to dig into their purses, wallets, and pockets one last time. Every man on board, from the quartermaster down to the humblest deck hand, would have spent the morning bowing and scraping to every passenger on ship in expectation of a generous reward of baksheesh.

On Christmas Day 1904, Mrs. Carson's trip up the Nile was done, but the crew of the *Rameses* had less than forty-eight hours on land, and then they would be Aswan-bound again.

EGYPT, ARABIA, AND SUDAN

"Our only fear is that her future passengers will be so completely spoiled for any other form of travelling that they will spend the remainder of their lives in vain and bitter comparisons." THE EGYPTIAN GAZETTE, 17 NOVEMBER 1911

John Mason Cook died on 6 March 1899. The cause of death according to one contemporary commentator was, "the too rigid performance of a task that overtaxed his failing powers." That task was organizing German emperor Wilhelm II's visit to the Holy Land in 1898.

The imperial party ran to over one hundred persons, escorted by twenty-seven Ottoman pashas with their eighty-strong entourage and six hundred Turkish troops. The exertions of providing for such an army overstretched even John, who was debilitated by the heat and contracted dysentery. He sought to recuperate, as so many had before him, on the Nile, traveling not on a Cook & Son steamer but on the emperor's own imperial yacht, the *Hohenzollern*. However, his conditioned worsened and he headed back home to England, where he died soon after. Thomas had passed away a few years previously, in 1892, at the age of 84—John had failed to make it back from Norway in time for the funeral.

With the death of its two figureheads, the business was now in the hands of John's sons, Frank (born 1862) and Ernest (born 1865). Bert (born 1867), who had at one time been heavily involved in the operations in Egypt, sold out to his brothers and retreated to the life of a country lord in England.

Mark Twain wrote that "[John Mason Cook] took the secret of how to handle a travel agency to his grave," after the company managed to lose all his luggage on a journey from America to Sweden but, in fact, the transition from one generation to the next was smooth. Thomas's grandsons had been involved in the day-to-day affairs of Cook & Son since they were in their teens: Frank had been in charge of business worldwide since the 1880s, and Ernest looked after the banking. Anyway, the real running of the company was in the hands of a vast corps of experienced managers and clerks who efficiently conducted the business like a well-drilled civil service. The firm was popularly said to be among the "three most competent organizations in the world"—the other two being the Roman Catholic Church and the Prussian Army.

OPPOSITE A passenger is assisted onto the Cook & Son steamer *Ambigole*. She flies an American flag, which suggests she has been hired out to a private party

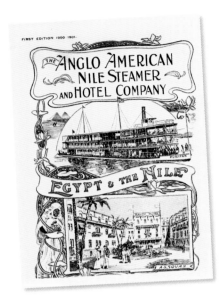

ABOVE The cover of the very first "Egypt & the Nile" brochure issued by the new Anglo-American Nile Steamer and Hotel Company for the season 1900–1901

OPPOSITE A rather more beautiful design issued by the same company from a few years later

Intrepid in their own right, both Frank and Ernest had journeyed to Persia in 1889, covering a thousand miles on horseback while investigating the country's possibilities for tourism, and a teenage Frank had led parties across Egypt's Sinai desert and up into what is now Jordan. Perhaps as a statement of intent, not long after John's death the company launched one of its most ambitious (and expensive) tours ever, which was a journey up the Nile to Khartoum, then south to Lake Victoria, Nairobi, and Mombasa. Frank, in particular, had a strong interest in Egypt and the company continued to promote the country as the resort for the "élite of fashionable society of every nation." However, they were no longer alone in this.

Since the late 1880s, when Cook & Son had built its own flotilla, thereby annulling its exclusive partnership with the khedive's administration, the way had been clear for others to launch their own Nile services. First to grasp the opportunity was the Tewfikiya Nile Navigation Company, which launched a sizeable fleet, including the large steamers *Al-Kahireh*, *Al-Khedive*, *and Memphis*, and the smaller *Dendareh*, *Edfou*, *Elephantine*, *Luxor*, *Philae*, and *Shellal*. It was managed by Alexander Rostovitz,★ who until recently had been John Cook's right-hand man on the Nile. Further twisting the knife, the main agent for the Tewfikiya was Cook's main rival in global travel, Henry Gaze & Son. However, the Tewfikiya boats were generally regarded as being much inferior to those of Cook & Son.

A more serious rival was the Anglo-American Nile Steamer and Hotel Company, set up in 1896, and which by 1900 had a fleet of three first-class steamers in the *Mayflower*, *Puritan*, and *Victoria*; three smaller steamers (the *Columbia*, *Indiana*, and *Niagara*); two launches (*Courlis* and *Witch*); and a small fleet of *dahabiya*s. The company's boats were distinctive: they were all sternwheelers and whereas Cook's steamers had a lower deck housed within the hull, the Anglo-American's had triple decks sat on top of a hull that was little more than a floating platform. The intent was to reduce the width and draft of the boats and so minimize the chances of running aground.

While not the most elegant fleet on the Nile—the top-heavy Anglo-American boats were ungainly going on ugly—the design seems to have paid off: Lilian Bell, a Chicago-born novelist and feminist, sailed on the *Mayflower* in 1900 and reported with some satisfaction of seeing one of Cook's big *Rameses* boats stuck on a sandbank "while we tooted past her blowing whistles of defiance and derision." She also reported

★ A keen acquirer of antiquities, Rostovitz would later bequeath a collection of 2,237 objects to the National Archaeological Museum in Athens.

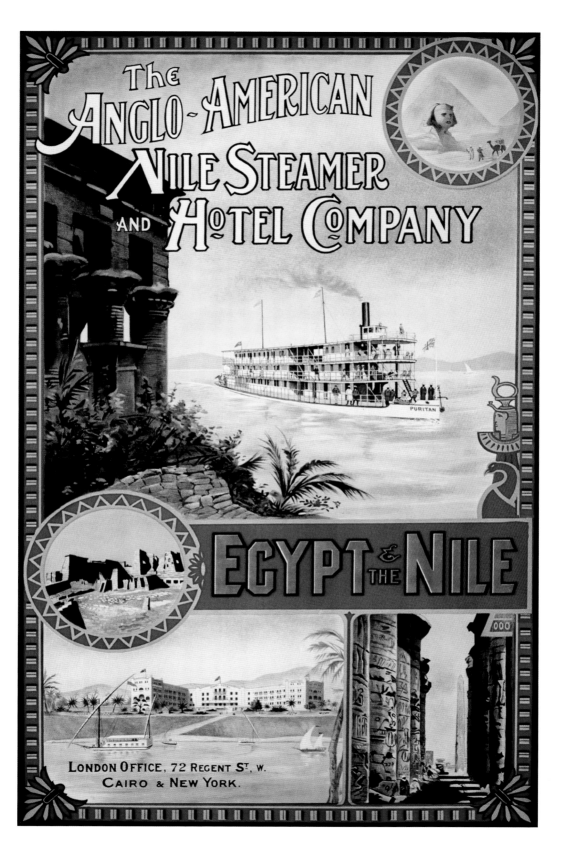

passing another, unidentified boat stuck fast, with all its bedding and stores piled up on the bank, and the passengers being ferried off in feluccas. "Whenever we felt ourselves going aground on a sandbank," she wrote, "we just reversed the engines and backed off again, or else put on extra steam and ground our way through it. In the whole three weeks we were not aground five minutes."

The patriotic Bell admitted to booking with Anglo-American because its boats were the only ones in Egypt that flew the American flag. On boarding, she was indignant "beyond words" then to see a huge Union Jack at the top of the forward flagstaff and beneath it only a tiny American flag. She demanded parity at the very least and was rewarded at Asyut with an enormous American flag, which had arrived by rail, and which was attached to the mast and hoisted twenty feet higher than the British flag.

The Anglo-American was able to offer weekly departures from Cairo during the season, with connecting services to the Second Cataract and through bookings to Khartoum. It promoted the option of a service that could take passengers from Cairo to Aswan and back again in eight days, which was faster and cheaper than anything Cook offered. This was made possible by using the overnight train from Cairo to Luxor, arriving mid-morning for a post-lunch sailing that reached Aswan in thirty-six hours, with brief stops at Edfu, Esna, and Kom Ombo; a full day in Aswan was followed by a daybreak departure that would have passengers back in Luxor that same night or early the following morning for two or three days of sightseeing before returning north by train.

In 1900, the Anglo-American also went head-to-head with Cook in the land-based hospitality business, opening its own hotel, the Savoy, on the northern tip of Elephantine Island at Aswan.

The company was strengthened in 1906 by amalgamation with the transatlantic Hamburg America Line, becoming in the process the Hamburg and Anglo-American Nile Company. Investment came in the form of two new, large steamers, the *Germania* and *Nubia*. The fleet now flew the German flag in addition to the Stars and Stripes.★

In the first years of the twentieth century, the Hamburg America Line was also increasing its sailings from Europe to Alexandria, notably with

In 1906 the Anglo-American amalgamated with the transatlantic Hamburg America Line to become the Hamburg and Anglo-American Nile Company

---

★ The appearance of German flags on the Nile was regarded with consternation in London, not just at Cook & Son's head office but in the corridors of Westminster, where the move—allied with the recent opening of a newly formed Deutsche Orient Bank in Cairo—was viewed as a plot to undermine British influence in Egypt and advance Germany's own interests in the region.

the addition of a new weekly 'express' service from Naples to Alexandria operated by the sleek, twin-screw *SS Oceana*. This was a result, in part, of the increasing popularity of Egypt with vacationing Americans, many of whom took the company's ships over from New York.

This state of affairs no doubt played a part in encouraging the formation of yet another new Nile-cruise venture, the American-operated Express Nile Navigation Company, which inaugurated services aboard its two purpose-built steamers, the *America* and the *Virginia*, in 1906. Its particular selling point was price: the company claimed its boats were the fastest on the Nile, with an average speed upstream of twelve knots an hour. This enabled them to sail Cairo–Aswan–Cairo in eight days as opposed to Cook & Son's standard twenty, with a corresponding significant reduction in cost. Tearing up and back down the Nile at breakneck speed was not, however, the experience most tourists were looking for and it is likely the Express Nile Navigation Company did not remain in business long—very little evidence of it exists.

Commentators predicted a price war on the Nile between fleets flying British, American, and German flags. Cook's response was not as expected. To stay ahead of the proliferating competition, the company elected not to cut prices but, instead, to upgrade its offerings, surpassing its rivals' new fleets with new boats of its own.

So it was that in the second week of December 1907, Cook & Son's first new luxury Nile steamer in almost twenty years, the *Egypt*, made its maiden voyage from Cairo to Aswan. It was, according to a correspondent of *The Egyptian Gazette*, "on a plane far above anything that has been known on

The Anglo-American boats looked markedly different from those of Cook & Son: they had decks that sat atop an incredibly shallow hull, giving them a top-heavy profile

Fifteen years after the last major addition to the Cook & Son fleet, which had been *Rameses the Third* in 1893, the *Egypt* represented a new level of luxury on the Nile

the Nile." No bigger than the existing Rameses boats,★ it was however more spacious, with lower decks that were high-ceilinged enough for a tall man not to have to stoop. It was also more luxurious: cabins were equipped with large wardrobes, folding tables, marble-topped wash stands, comfortable armchairs, and spring-mattress beds. The boat was fitted out, commented the *Gazette*, "with the comforts of an ocean-going liner." Another journalist called the *Egypt* "the *Mauretania* of the Nile," a reference to the Cunard Line's new Atlantic ocean liner, the largest and fastest in the world, which had launched just two and a half months previously.

Three seasons later, in 1911, the *Egypt* was joined by a sister vessel, the *Arabia*. The two boats were built (by the Thornycroft shipyard of Southampton, England) to the same design, although the *Arabia* was about six feet longer, with a slight difference in the arrangement of cabins. Both had sixteen single-berth cabins and four cabins de luxe on the upper deck, another twenty-two single-berth cabins on the main deck, and a further eight double-berth cabins and eight single-berth cabins on the lower deck. Cabins for stewards and stewardesses were also on the lower deck, along with the kitchen, cold store, and a refrigerating plant.

The boats were steered from a chart- and wheelhouse right forward on top of the promenade deck. The engine room was amidships on the main

★ The size of the steamers was restricted by the shallowness of the Nile and by having to pass through several sets of barrages (locks) on the Nile, including at Asyut, Nag' Hammadi, and Esna; the maximum width the locks could accommodate was around fifty feet. As a consequence, even the largest of the Nile steamers was never as grand or carried as many passengers as the great American river steamers on which they were modeled.

deck, with the boats powered by a set of triple-diagonal surface-condensing engines, manufactured by Inglis & Co. of Glasgow, which delivered 500 horsepower. The steam was supplied by two locomotive boilers, each six foot six inches in diameter. The paddle wheels were ten foot six inches in diameter. Both were fitted with a steam windlass forward and a steam capstan aft for use in removing themselves from sandbanks.

A luncheon was given aboard the *Arabia* at Cairo on 17 November, to which a host of local dignitaries and correspondents were invited. The *Gazette* was effusive in its praise:

> The passenger accommodation of the *Arabia* is quite of the most delectable and luxurious order imaginable. Upon the upper deck is the spacious dining salon panelled in pale green enamelled wood and most comfortably furnished with small tables. There is also a delightfully dainty drawing room with grey panelled walls, and the prettiest cretonne covered chairs and lounges, and dainty little writing tables beneath the windows, and card tables and many other devices for whiling away the passing hour. Forward of this is an equally comfortable observation saloon sheltered from the head wind by large glazed windows; and the smoking saloon with its quiet toned furnishings of fumed oak offers an absolute refuge of rest to the votaries of the goddess Nicotine.

Three years after the arrival of the *Egypt*, she was joined by a near-identical sister vessel, the *Arabia*

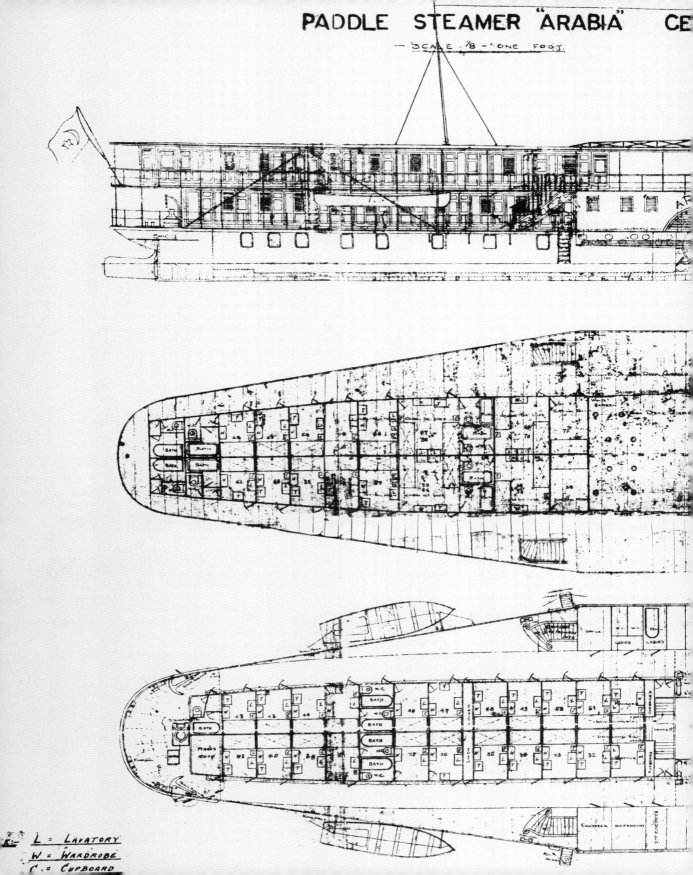

SCALE ⅛ - ONE FOOT

L = LAVATORY
W = WARDROBE
C = CUPBOARD

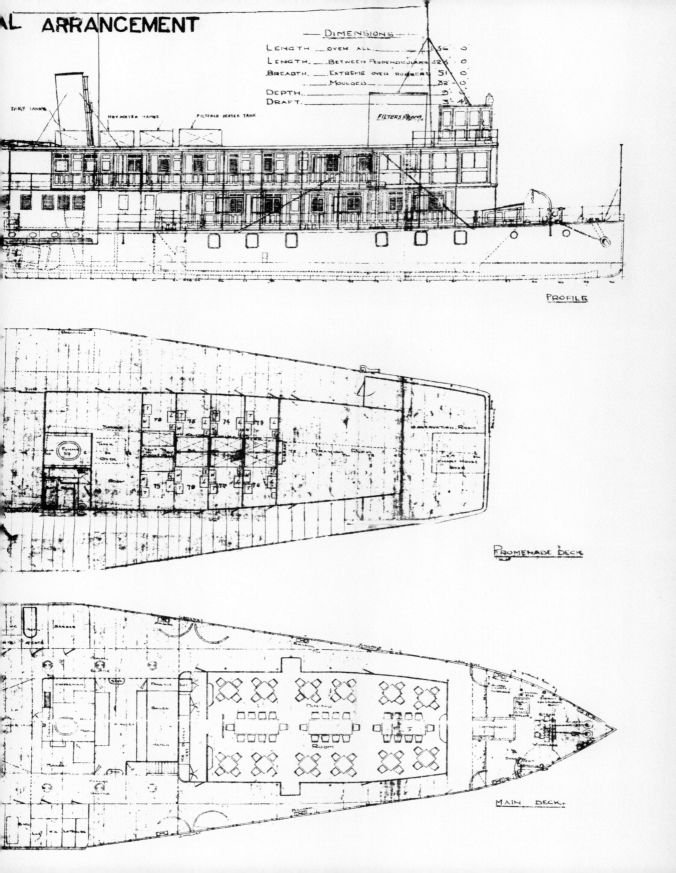

AL ARRANGEMENT

DIMENSIONS

LENGTH ... OVER ALL 156 0
LENGTH ... BETWEEN PERPENDICULARS 128 0
BREADTH ... EXTREME OVER RUBBERS 51 0
         ... MOULDED 32 0
DEPTH 9 0
DRAFT 3 4

TANKS TANKS   HOT WATER TANKS   FILTERED WATER TANK   FILTERS ROOM

PROFILE

PROMENADE DECK

MAIN DECK

PREVIOUS SPREAD Original engineering blueprints for the *Arabia*, drawn up by John Thornycroft & Company of Southampton

ABOVE A swish if over-furnished bedroom suite and lounge aboard the *Egypt*

OPPOSITE Formerly Austrian Lloyd, the company's name was changed to Lloyd Triestino in 1919, when Trieste became a part of Italy. It ran weekly services from Genoa, Trieste, and Venice to Alexandria

The cabins throughout are extraordinarily commodious and airy, the patent window frames allowing for plenty of light and ventilation, and the same scheme of decoration and furnishing being observed throughout. There is also roomy accommodation for private ladies' maids, for whose convenience too has been fitted up a private dining salon in the stern of the boat. There is also on board a well equipped hair dressing salon where face massage, manicure, electric massage, etc, can be procured at the hands of a very skilful master of his art.

Indeed from an inspection of the *Arabia* at her moorings and a participation in the most excellent luncheon most dextrously served on Friday, our only fear is that her future passengers will be so completely spoiled for any other form of travelling that they will spend the remainder of their lives in vain and bitter comparisons.

The *Arabia* departed Cairo on her maiden voyage to Aswan on Tuesday 21 November 1911. Cook & Son's fleet now ran to nine first-class steamers, four Express steamers, seven small steamers, and numerous *dahabiya*s. At any given time during the season, the company might have somewhere around seven hundred passengers on the Nile.

Still demand grew and less than three years later an order for yet another boat was made. With only the hull completed, construction was suddenly stopped—the shipyard had other, more pressing obligations because on 14 August 1914 war had broken out in Europe.

No battles were fought in Egypt during the First World War, but the country was a mustering station for troops destined for campaigns in

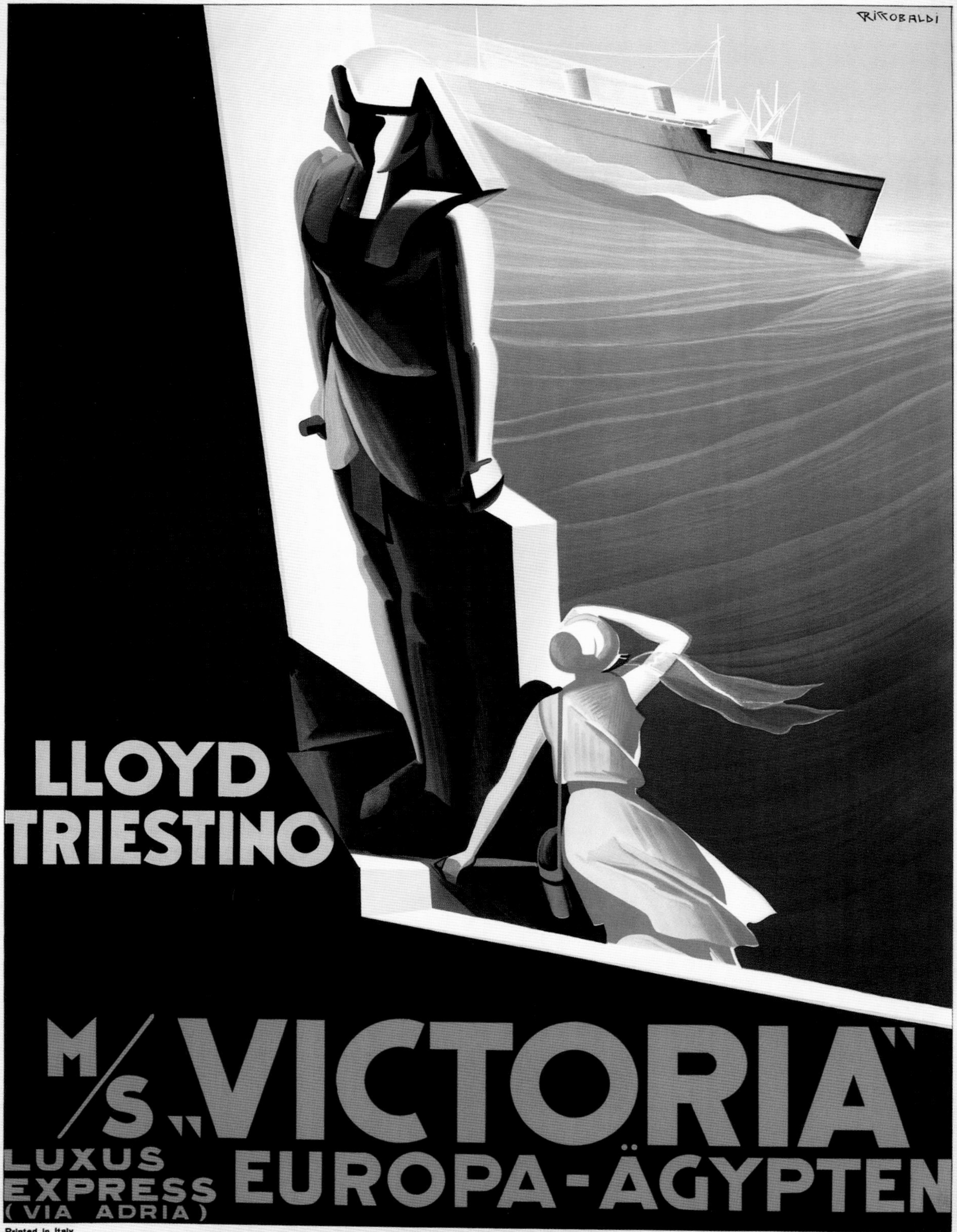

Courtesy Galleria L'Image, original vintage posters – Alassio, Italy

neighboring Palestine. And from 1915, the wounded from the Dardanelles campaign were shipped into Alexandria to be hospitalized there or in Cairo, and then in many cases possibly sent off up the Nile to recuperate. Although the season 1913–14 had been a busy one for the operators of Nile tourist steamers, in the fall of 1914 Cook & Son's *Travellers' Gazette* (the successor to *The Excursionist*) was regretfully announcing the postponement of the usual season until the New Year. In fact, the tourist business in Egypt would be stopped for the next six years.

Cairo was compensated by the large numbers of troops from Britain and all over the world who poured into the city and were billeted in sprawling camps in the suburbs, including at the Pyramids. The soldiers' spending more than made up for the loss of the usual visitors. Luxor and Aswan were not so fortunate, as the troops were not given enough free time to allow them to travel to the south. Instead, these towns were filled with the wounded, some of whom were billeted at the Winter Palace, which had been turned into a hospital. Aswan was even more of a city of the dead: its large hotels, the Cataract and the Savoy, were closed for the duration.

For the first year of the war, Cook & Son kept the steamers running on its Express and Second Cataract services for the benefit of freight and native passengers, but owing to the high wartime cost of coal, the former service was stopped in late 1915. In December the British government commandeered the four express steamers *Amenartas*, *Cleopatra*, *Hatasoo*, and *Nefertari*, along with six first-class steamers, *Amasis* (formerly the *Prince Mohammed Ali*), *Prince Abbas*, *Rameses*, *Rameses the Great*, *Rameses the Third*, and *Tewfik*. For

OPPOSITE Rotterdamsche Lloyd's main trade was with Java, but its boats called at Port Said and Suez en route

LEFT One of Cook's steamers undergoing conversion prior to sailing for Mesopotamia; the upper decks have been removed and high armor plating is being fixed around the bows

PREVIOUS SPREAD AND ABOVE Passengers disembark the steamer *Sudan* to run a gauntlet of souvenir sellers. The location of the photo on the previous spread is unknown but the scene above is Esna, identifiable by the barrage in the background

several weeks the boats underwent refitting in Egypt: all the upper decks and cabins were dismantled because instead of sixty to eighty passengers the boats were now intended to carry six hundred to eight hundred troops, bunked down on bare boards. The sponsons that enclosed the paddle wheels and, in some cases, the paddle wheels themselves were also removed, so that the boats (which had to be towed) could pass through the barrages north of Cairo. Around 248 million tons of water was released from the Aswan Dam to make sure the otherwise shallow northern reaches of the river were deep enough for the boats to navigate. Once through the barrages, the boats were rebuilt and stiffened with longitudinal girders to help them stand up to the rigors of a proposed 3,500-mile sea voyage. They now proceeded under their own steam to Rosetta, on the coast, where the sandbar had been dredged to allow passage out onto the Mediterranean. Once in the open sea, they picked up an escort to Port Said, where they were dry-docked and their engines and boilers given an overhaul.

Toward the end of February 1916 the little Nile steamer fleet departed Suez with crews brought over from England, supplemented with Somali sailors and firemen. It arrived in Basra at the beginning of March, from where some of the boats were immediately dispatched with stores and troops north to Amara on the Tigris. They would all serve in the Mesopotamia campaign being fought against the Turks; none would return. Three of the boats were lost even before the operation began, destroyed by fire on 5 January 1916 while at dock at Bulaq in Cairo.

Payment had not been agreed in advance and when Cook & Son billed the British government £226,489 for the loss of its boats, the claim was decried in internal Foreign Office correspondence as "grotesque, if not to say dishonest." The government countered with its own valuation of £73,842, and that, after volumes of correspondence between the two parties, is what Frank Cook reluctantly settled for, plus a £17,000 insurance payout on the three boats destroyed by fire.

Cook & Son cannot have been too aggrieved at the settlement because in 1918 it permitted six more steamers to be released to the military. The Anglo-American Company also had some of its boats pressed into service, including both the *Indiana* and *Niagara*, which were put to work on the Suez Canal as hospital ships, ferrying soldiers wounded in Palestine from the railhead at Qantara up to the hospitals at Port Said.

When the war ended in November 1918, the world needed time to recover. Egypt's occupation by foreign troops had also triggered pro-independence unrest, which was regularly spilling over into violence on the streets. For these reasons, it wasn't until late in 1920 that Cook & Son was able to announce to the world the resumption of its world-famous Nile steamboat services, starting January 1921.

In comparison with pre-war seasons, the services were now considerably restricted, mainly owing to the fact that so many of the company's steamers were gone. In terms of first-class tourists steamers, all that was left were *Egypt* and *Arabia*, and a new addition to the fleet, the *Thebes*, which made its maiden voyage that January.

Another vessel was added the following month. This was the boat that had been commissioned before the war and had only now been finished. Built once again by Thornycroft of Southampton as a sister vessel to *Egypt* and *Arabia*, the new boat was named *Sudan*. It made its maiden voyage from Cairo, bound for Aswan, on 8 February 1921, taking over sailings originally intended for the *Arabia*, which had been chartered for a full six weeks by His Highness Fu'ad I, Sultan of Egypt.

Although no one could have suspected it at the time, *Sudan* was the last first-class steamer to be added to Cook & Son's Nile fleet.

DEATH ON THE NILE

"Death on the Nile seems to define not just Agatha Christie but some essential element of Nile romance." ROBERT TWIGGER, 2013

As the calendar rolled over into the 1920s, the prospects for Nile tourism were encouraging. Cook & Son had its three new first-class steamers, the *Egypt*, *Arabia*, and *Sudan*, recently supplemented by the purchase of two sternwheelers that had originally been commissioned by the British government for service in Mesopotamia but, with the end of the war, had become surplus to requirements. Named the *Damietta* and *Rosetta*, both were capable of carrying sixty passengers. There was also the *Thebes*, which operated the Second Cataract service. In addition, the company had a fleet of eight small, private steamers (*Chonsu*, *Fostat*, *Memnon*, *Nitocris*, *Oonas*, *Scarab*, *Serapis*, and *Seti*) and six *dahabiya*s.

The Anglo-American Nile Company had, unsurprisingly, severed its links with the German-owned Hamburg America Line and had instead entered into partnership with the American Express Company, which was acting as its global agent, selling tickets for berths aboard its five large Nile steamers.

If it had been slow to pick up in the wake of the Great War, the Nile cruise business found itself rapidly propelled to full speed not long after, with the catalyst being the most amazing of archaeological discoveries.

It was only as recently as 1912 that American excavator Theodore Davis had declared, "The Valley of the Kings is now exhausted." He had passed on his concession to dig in the area to the English Lord Carnarvon, who hired one of Davis's former collaborators, Howard Carter, to continue the work. Carnarvon financed the dig in the Valley of the Kings until it was interrupted by the First World War, after which Carter resumed his work. After several more years without result, Carnarvon informed Carter that he had one more season before the funding would be stopped. On 4 November 1922, Carter uncovered a set of steps leading to a tomb entrance with seals intact. He immediately wired his benefactor and then waited patiently for a fortnight, until Carnarvon reached Luxor on the twenty-third. The antechamber to the tomb was entered six days later, and the first reports of the find were carried in *The Times* of London the following day, 30 November. So began

OPPOSITE Disembarking the *Thebes*, a small stern-wheel steamer, used by Cook & Son on the Second Cataract service between Aswan and Wadi Halfa

the second reign of Tutankhamun, three thousand years after his death. In the coming weeks, half the world followed Carnarvon to Luxor, everyone from the queen of Belgium to the mayor of New York. The hotels were full and the managers had to resort to erecting tents in their gardens to meet demand, while the riverside Corniche was jammed with moored *dahabiya*s.

In a world recently emerged from war, the discovery of the tomb was a rare tonic, a fabulous story that combined adventure, exoticism, and heaps of real treasure.* Then there was the added drama of Carnarvon's death just five months after the opening of the tomb, ostensibly from blood poisoning, the result of a septic mosquito bite, but so much more intriguing to attribute it to the wrath of a long-dead pharaoh. No wonder Tutankhamun captured the global imagination. Maynard Owen Williams was in Luxor for *National Geographic*, and in May 1923 the town was still full of excited visitors trying to get in on the biggest story of the decade: "We came in the glory of late afternoon to the gray bund of Luxor, alive with tourists from the big hotels and from three steamers which had just arrived. I stepped into a shop to leave my films and realized that the sway of Tutankhamen still grips the world, for a woman in white was speaking: 'I do hope that we can get a pass, because I'm just crazy over mummies, and they say this one will be the best of all.'"

The story ran for years and ensured that there wasn't an empty cabin on a Nile cruise for years to come. The English novelist Rudyard Kipling, author

OPPOSITE Tourists sit out on the terrace of the Winter Palace, on what appears to be an uncharacteristically cold day for Luxor judging by the heavy dress

ABOVE LEFT The Winter Palace as seen from Cook & Son's moorings at Luxor

ABOVE A German version of Cook & Son's Egypt brochure, still playing on the Tutankhamun find seven years later

---

* Later, when the treasures had been removed from the tomb and catalogued, they were sent down to Cairo aboard barges towed by a Cook & Son tug and delivered to the company's wharf by the Qasr al-Nil Bridge.

of *Kim* and *The Jungle Book,* was a passenger aboard the *Egypt* in March 1929. In a letter to his daughter, he writes of finding Luxor busy with steamers, his vessel being just one of a string vying for moorings: "and now the Cairo boat, going north, has just pulled out, yelling like a real liner."

Almost as much welcome publicity for the Nile cruise (in the long term, perhaps more) came from the discovery of more dead bodies, although this time around they were a lot fresher. Agatha Christie was already a best-selling crime writer when her twenty-second novel, *Death on the Nile*, was published in the United Kingdom in November 1937. Although forever associated with an England of vicarages and afternoon teas, Christie had a love for the Middle East. She first visited in 1910–11, accompanying her mother, who had been advised by a doctor to seek a warm climate in which to recuperate from illness. The pair sailed from Marseilles on the *Heliopolis*, belonging to the British-owned Egyptian Mail Company, and installed themselves at Cairo's Gezira Palace hotel for three months. The twenty-year-old Agatha Miller, as she was, spent the time watching polo and the races at the neighboring Gezira Sports Club, and attending dances and parties. She stubbornly ignored any attempts to distract her with visits to the museum or a trip up the Nile. It wasn't until nineteen years later, when she married her second husband, the archaeologist Max Mallowan, that she developed an interest in antiquity. Mallowan dug in eastern Syria and Iraq, where his wife was a regular visitor and enthusiastic helper. The trips provided material for several books: *Murder in Mesopotamia* (1936) takes place at a dig in Iraq; *Murder on the Orient Express* (1934) was born out of her own experience being stranded on a train when heavy rains washed away the track; while in *Appointment with Death* (1938), murder takes place at the ancient site of Petra in Jordan.

In 1933, Agatha revisited Egypt and took a Nile cruise with Max and Rosalind, the daughter from her first marriage. They played chess with Howard Carter in the lobby of the Winter Palace at Luxor, and encountered a fellow passenger whom Agatha and Rosalind found domineering to the point of sadism, and who was the inspiration for Mrs. Boynton, the former prison wardress in *Appointment with Death*. At Aswan, rather than return directly to Cairo, the evidence suggests they continued on to the Second Cataract—the evidence being that the events that play out in Christie's Nile murder novel take place on the river between the First and Second Cataracts.

After a prologue in England, and a brief stop-off at the Mena House hotel in Cairo, the cast of *Death on the Nile* is brought together at the Cataract hotel in Aswan, which Christie herself obviously visited, although there is no evidence to say she ever stayed there: passengers on Nile cruises kept their

Tourists saddled up for the ride to the Valley of the Kings; ties were obviously required when visiting royal tombs

Agatha Christie and husband, the archaeologist Max Mallowan, on board a Nile steamer while holidaying in Egypt in either 1931 or 1933

cabins while visiting Aswan. No matter that she was on holiday, Christie remained sharply observant and *Death on the Nile* knowingly portrays the western tourist on the Nile. Her excursionists are reliably snooty about the "awful crowd" disembarking from some other steamer, and cynically dismiss the souvenirs on offer as all being shipped in from Europe; dragomans drone, while the German doctor has his head buried in a Baedeker.

In the book, the steamer that neatly serves to keep the characters confined to a single set is called the *Karnak*. It's an invention—the only boat on the Nile of that name had been part of the Tewfikiya Nile Navigation Company fleet in the 1880s and it's unlikely to have still been in service by the 1930s. The likelihood is that the fictional vessel was based on Cook & Son's *Thebes*. This is the boat that ran the Second Cataract service at this time, and the annotated deck plan Christie includes in her book, to identify which character occupied which cabin, is almost identical to that of the *Thebes*.

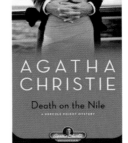

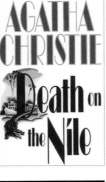

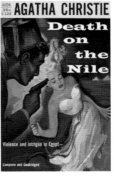

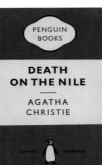

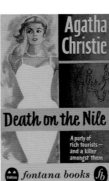
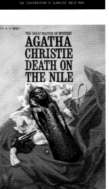

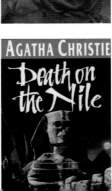

The Nubian stretch of the Nile is well suited to Christie's murderous schemes because it is barely inhabited, with no towns or villages, just desert, mountains, and what she describes as "a melancholy, almost sinister charm."

Cook's services departed Shellal mid-afternoon, sailing for a few hours before mooring for the night. On the second day, the steamers passed through the gorge of Kalabsha before halting at Gerf Hussein to visit a rock temple built by Ramesses II, and then sailing again until reaching Wadi al-Sebua, or the "Valley of the Lions"—Christie has her characters conversing while walking up the avenue of sphinxes here. The following day, after breakfast, the boat would arrive at Amada, with a shore visit to its small temple dating from the time of Tutmosis III, but the main event came later that day toward sunset, when the Temple of Abu Simbel came into view.

Helen Mary Tirard, visiting more than forty years before Christie, imbued the approach with some atmosphere:

> We went forward at a great rate, and at 9.30 p.m. we saw the front of the great temple, with its wonderful colossi looking far down the river towards us. Through our glasses we could distinguish their features, and could see that, though they were looking down the river, they were not looking at us at all; they were looking far beyond us, though we were still so far from them. We could not realize what they were looking for or at, for to our eyes, down the river behind us there seemed to be nothing; they appeared to be watching something intently, something of which we had no consciousness. Soon we were close under them, the *Sethi* at anchor, and we on shore.

In *Death on the Nile*, the *Karnak* must arrive in darkness because its passengers wake the following morning surprised to discover the temple alongside the boat. In reality, even passengers whose boats arrived after sundown could hardly have missed seeing the temple because around 1900 Cook & Son had paid for and helped install powerful electric lights to illuminate the façade by night. Christie made Abu Simbel the site of an attempt on a life by means of a bouncing boulder.

Only a morning was spent here, before at 11 a.m. the boat would be underway again to reach the service's southern terminus of Wadi Halfa that same afternoon. This was Sudan. Some passengers may have been continuing onward, linking with the train-de-luxe, which left each evening at 8 p.m., taking twenty-seven hours to reach Khartoum. Otherwise, after overnighting at Wadi Halfa, the next afternoon the boat would begin its return journey

PREVIOUS SPREAD The *Thebes*, the likely model for the *Karnak* in *Death on the Nile*, passes below the Cataract hotel at Aswan, which also features in the novel

ABOVE A poster advertising the Wagons-Lits' London-to-Cairo rail service

OPPOSITE The first edition of *Death on the Nile*, published in 1937, featured a stylized painting of a steamer at Abu Simbel, seen here (top row, third from left) with some of the hundreds of international editions of the book published since then

The Wagons-Lits sleeper *Star of Egypt* at Aswan. The train offered a far faster and cheaper, and scarcely less luxurious alternative to travel between Cairo and Upper Egypt

north, making another stop at Abu Simbel—in Christie's novel the second halt at Abu Simbel heralds a second, more successful murder attempt. One further day's sailing would have everybody back at Shellal to connect with the Cairo boat, which would be departing Aswan the following day.

Christie's whodunit represents a last hurrah of the Nile steamers. By the time of her own voyage, the services were already in decline. Five years before, in February 1928, Frank and Ernest Cook had sold the family firm to the Compagnie Internationale des Wagons-Lits of Belgium for the sum of £3.5 million. The reasons for the sale are unknown, but it is possible that the brothers, who were by now in their sixties, simply wanted to retire from the business.

Wagons-Lits was best known as the operator of the famed Orient Express. The company was founded in the 1870s by George Nagelmackers, son of the banker to King Leopold of Belgium. He started with the idea of providing luxurious railway carriages—"palaces on wheels"—and, assisted by royal patronage, he spread his carriages, sleeping cars, and restaurant cars throughout Europe and beyond. In 1898, the company had moved into Egypt, launching a luxury train service on the Cairo–Aswan line. The trains featured sleeping cars and a dining car cooled by air blown over three hundred pounds of ice. Wagons-Lits increasingly became Cook's chief competitor in the Egyptian travel business, offering tourists the option of reaching the monuments of Luxor and Aswan speedily and comfortably without going on the river at all. Through a subsidiary, the Compagnie Internationale des Grands Hôtels, it also added luxury hotels to its Egyptian portfolio; in 1894, the C.I.G.H. had bought the Gezira Palace and, two years later, took ownership of Shepheard's.

As far as Frank and Ernest were concerned, the sale to Wagons-Lits was a shrewd one, or, at least, extremely lucky. The Wall Street crash of the following year practically meant the disappearance of the American traveler abroad, and kept much of Europe at home too. According to Cook & Son historian Piers Brendon, between 1929 and 1931 Cook's saw forty-five per cent of its business vanish. The fallout in Egypt was that, in order to cut costs, Cook & Son began reducing the size of its Nile fleet: twelve ships were sold, mainly for scrap, between 1934 and 1939. It did not help that new owner Wagons-Lits was keen to shift people onto its new sleeper trains, the Birmingham-built *Star of Egypt* and *Sunshine Express*, at the expense of the steamers. Wagons-Lits advertising highlighted that by train it was just twelve hours from Cairo to Luxor for a cost of around £4 in a sleeping car, with the fare to Aswan costing just a pound more; contrast that with £65 and an investment of twenty days for a standard Nile cruise.

Any chance that tourism on the Nile might bounce back was put paid to by the outbreak once more of war in Europe. This time the conflict did reach Egypt: if not Cairo and the Nile Valley, at least as far as the desert and al-Alamein. Cook's remaining steamers were once again used for war purposes. Some, notably the *Arabia*, were used as floating billets and officers' clubs; others, including the *Damietta* and *Rosetta*, were sold off to the British Army. Only Cook's Bulaq shipyard was kept busy, constructing light coastal craft for the British Navy. In fact, even before the war began the company made more money from its engineering services at Bulaq than it did from the few steamers that were kept running.

The steamer services had weathered wars before; the firm of Cook & Son, in particular, had survived the loss of its whole tourist-carrying fleet in the Sudan campaigns and ten further boats in the First World War. There seemed no good reason not to believe that, once hostilities ended, the leisurely pastime of exploring Egypt from the decks of a Nile steamer would resume once more. Sadly, this was not to be the case.

Soldiers aboard the requisitioned Cook & Son steamer *Thebes* during the Second World War, from the photo album of G.J. Mostert, SAAF 15 Squadron

THE RIVER AFTER STEAM

"There is a timelessness to life on the river that belies the momentous events sweeping the country." TOBY WILKINSON, 2012

After the First World War ended it took only two or three years for the tourists to return to Egypt and for the likes of Cook & Son to resume Nile passenger services. When the Second World War finished it took considerably longer—the best part of twenty years, in fact.

In the immediate aftermath there was optimism and Cook & Son was keen to resume operations. In this it had the support of the British government, which expressed the opinion that tourism would return to Egypt and when it did "it would be best if a British company could collect some of the profits." (During the Second World War, Wagons-Lits, with its headquarters in enemy-occupied Belgium, had its share capital in Cook & Son annulled, and the company reverted to being wholly British-owned.)

But while peace settled on Europe, the same was not true of the Middle East. There was war between the Arab states, Egypt included, and the newly declared state of Israel in 1948, which went badly and which fed back into the violence that would burn Egypt's own path to independence just a few years later. Management at Cook & Son's London headquarters revised its view on the company's future in Egypt and took the decision to sell off what remained of the fleet, including the *Arabia*, *Egypt*, *Sudan*, and *Thebes*, as well as the smaller *Delta*, *Fostat*, and *Memnon*, all of which went to private buyers, mostly Egyptian landowners and aristocracy, between late 1948 and March 1950.

Just as we have Miss Riggs's diary documenting Thomas Cook's very first Nile cruise in February 1869, we also have a dispatch from, if not the last ever Cook & Son steamer sailing, certainly one of the last. The writer and aesthete Roderick Cameron went up the Nile aboard the *Memnon* in September 1948. This was just a month before she would be sold to the statesman Ali Maher Pasha, who had served two terms as Egyptian prime minister and would serve twice more, in 1952; he purchased the steamer in October 1948 for use as his personal houseboat. Before then, however, Cameron and his party chartered the *Memnon* to sail to Aswan and back over

An unidentified former Cook & Son steamer near Abu Simbel, on Lake Nasser, in 1965

three weeks. He was not unaware of the political situation—"The British ascendancy in Egypt is already a thing of the past. We are not popular"—but he was reassured by the talismanic authority still wielded by the company to which he had entrusted himself: "the political situation does not seem to have affected Thomas Cook & Son's position in the country. They are still all-powerful, a kind of East India Company of our time, nabobs of the Middle East."

Cameron described the *Memnon* as being "like an Edwardian country house evoked from the past, transplanted by chance to the Nile," and he was quite correct—built in 1903, the *Memnon* was of the Edwardian age. He described decks spread with carpet, and set with wicker chairs made comfortable with nests of cushions; woodwork that was white and brass that shone; beds spread with eiderdowns; and on all the writing desks, pens with clean nibs, engraved paper, and sealing wax. Before departing Cairo, Cameron's party stood on deck clinking whisky and sodas as speeches were made and they were wished a "bon voyage." "An onlooker might have thought us VIPS, big shots off on some nebulous mission of great importance. It was the kind of scene one sees flashed on the news reels, and as far as Thomas Cook & Son is concerned I suppose it was important, for ours was the first steamer to go up the Nile since the war."

While Cook & Son was making one last great effort to turn back the clock, the majority of Nile steamers were already pretty much permanently at anchor. In the late 1940s, a couple of the Anglo-American boats were moored at Rod al-Farag at Cairo, where they served as floating hotels for transiting passengers on the British Overseas Air Corporation's flying-boat services between Britain and South Africa. Some of the former Cook & Son boats now also served as floating hotels, operated by Egyptian tour companies. Like the *Memnon*, other boats became floating homes.

The Welsh newspaperman James Morris (later to become travel writer Jan Morris) lived aboard a moored steamer at Gezira in Cairo in the early 1950s. She was the *Saphir*, and where she came from we don't know, but Morris remembered her beautifully in a 1984 piece for *The New York Times*:

> …permanently moored beside the river bank but still ineffably nautical—tall, raked funnel amidships, engines shrouded down below, awnings everywhere against the sun and wheelhouse high above. She had a galley and a saloon, like any proper steamboat. She had staterooms and deck cabins and a big shady poop. And well forward on her upper deck, square, windowed all round, white-painted but a bit blistered by the heat, stood my workroom—the most glamorous room, the most suggestive and the most unforgettable that I have ever occupied.

> There was the dry, dazzling light of Egyptian sunshine, like no other on earth. There were the rippling reflections on my white ceiling of the majestic river outside. There were exotic smells—of cooking

The Anglo-American steamer *Mayflower*, moored at Cairo where she served as floating accommodation for passengers on African flying-boat services

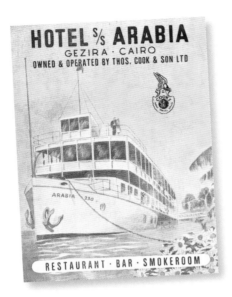

A brochure from possibly the late 1940s before the *Arabia* was sold into private hands when, for a short period, Cook & Son operated her as a floating hotel

oil, of wood fires, of fish, of earthy water, of insufficiently refined gasoline. And best of all there were sounds, wonderful sounds—the muffled roar and hooting of the city streets, of course, but also the creaking of timbers, the clanging of pots and pans, the chanting of the blind Koran singer who sat all day in his wicker chair along the road, and three times a day the miraculous call to prayer from the mosque across the river, eddying hauntingly over the water and through the trees, and answered as if in echo from countless minarets near and far across the capital. All around me the life of the great river proceeded, intimately close, so that as I sat there among my books I felt truly a part of it.

Sadly, returning to Cairo many years later Morris found only an empty mooring and, on asking around, discovered the *Saphir* had sunk.

Roderick Cameron's "Edwardian country house," meanwhile, was a regal residence house no longer—she became a floating dig house. The son of Ali Maher Pasha leased her to the University of Chicago to use as a mobile headquarters for the teams involved in the campaign to rescue the monuments of Nubia from the rising waters created by the construction of the High Dam. This was 1960 and by this time she hadn't sailed for twelve years; her engines had to be overhauled and she was fitted out with a new boiler, following which she very slowly made her way from Cairo to Aswan.

Keeping the *Memnon*'s engines fueled proved to be an expensive business and for the following seasons the scientists sought another less costly solution. They bought another boat, Cook & Son's old sternwheeler the *Fostat*, which they remodeled, stripping out its engines to provide more space for living and working quarters, and using a tug to move her around. After duty in the Nubian Salvage Campaign, the *Fostat* was returned to permanent moorings in Cairo, where she served until the late 1980s as the occasional residence for the director of the American Research Center in Egypt.

This was far from the first time Nile steamers were at the disposal of Egyptologists: back in the 1880s, the head of the Antiquities Service, Gaston Maspero, had his own "Museum steamer," which was both his home and his means of shuttling up and down the Nile to inspect the sites under his jurisdiction. J.P. Morgan, the financier who was also a president of New York's Metropolitan Museum of Art and instrumental in forming its Department of Egyptian Art, commissioned Cook & Son to build him his own steamer, around 1911–12, which he called the *Khargeh*. Unfortunately, he didn't have long to enjoy it as he died in 1913; what happened to his boat is unknown.

Ironically, it was the threatened loss of Egypt's Nubian monuments that finally brought the tourists back. International coverage of the rescue campaigns at Philae and Abu Simbel proved to be the best advertising imaginable and from the early 1960s onward the number of foreign visitors to Egypt began to climb. By the middle of the decade, for the first time in perhaps forty years, new Nile fleets were assembled. One of the companies leading the way was Hilton International, whose Nile Hilton, opened in 1959, had been the first major new hotel in Egypt since the 1920s; it introduced two new vessels, the *Isis* and the *Osiris*. This was the beginning of a period of incredible—and to a large extent uncontrollable—growth, which, by the end of the twentieth century, resulted in there being over 250 new cruise boats on the Nile. Even the restrictions introduced in the early 1990s on sailing between Cairo and Luxor because of political instability in Middle Egypt, which occasionally manifested itself in terrorists taking potshots at passing tourist boats, did nothing to dampen the new-found enthusiasm for the Nile; it just squashed all the boats into the 217-kilometer stretch of river between Luxor and Aswan. At the height of recent tourism in Egypt, in 2010, some 58,000 passengers sailed on Nile cruises. Thomas Cook's notions of democratizing travel to Egypt were well and truly realized.

What would he have made, then, of the fate of the sole surviving boat from the Cook & Son fleet? This is the *Sudan*, the last first-class passenger

A steamer passing Abu Simbel on its way to Wadi Halfa, in a dramatic painting by British artist Alan Sorrell made in 1962, at the time of Nubian Salvage Campaign

steamer to be built for the company, operating between Cairo and Aswan from February 1921 until the outbreak of war in 1939. After being used as a floating officers' club at Cairo, she was sold to Fuad Serageldin, secretary-general of Egypt's Wafd Party and holder of various cabinet posts in the 1940s until his political career was abruptly terminated by the Free Officers' coup; his boat was just one of the many things taken from him in the name of nationalization. She subsequently found her way into the possession of the Egyptian-owned Eastmar Line and was put back to work carrying tourists. At some later date she was taken on by the French tourism company Club Méditerranée, who moored her at Luxor as a floating hotel. In 2003 she was sold again, this time to the French travel outfit Voyageurs du Monde, who did the decent thing and restored her. As part of the refit, the new owners reduced the number of cabins from the original fifty-six, plus four suites, to eighteen far larger spaces plus five roomy suites, transforming her in the process into a distinctly luxurious vessel. Catering for the heritage, that is to say, very top end, of the travel market, the *Sudan* currently sails ten months of the year between Luxor and Aswan, with the occasional cruise between Cairo and Aswan (since 2013 a limited number of boats have been permitted to sail the full route of old, once again).

For those who cannot afford a cabin on the *Sudan*, her period charms are on display masquerading as the *Karnak* in the 2004 British television-film version of *Death on the Nile*, starring David Suchet as Inspector Poirot. (The starry 1978 cinema production, with Peter Ustinov as Poirot, employed the *Memnon*, another old Cook & Son steamer, now gutted and lying sawn in two, like a magic trick gone wrong, in a boatyard in Cairo.)

BELOW AND OPPOSITE The *Sudan*, which is now owned and operated by French travel company Voyageurs du Monde, offers the opportunity to experience the Nile in similar fashion to Cook & Son's passengers of a century ago

The *Sudan* is the only surviving Cook & Son boat but there are at least two other historic steamers still sailing the Nile.★ The small sternwheeler *Karim* was built in Great Britain, in 1917, for service in Mesopotamia. She may or may not have gotten there but after the First World War she ended up in Egypt, where she was purchased by the Egyptian government. She possibly did service as a royal yacht in the fleet belonging to King Fu'ad and later Faruq before being nationalized post-revolution. She then disappeared from sight until 1991, when she was purchased by a local tourist operator, Spring Tours. She has since been used for Nile cruises, marketed internationally by various luxury companies, although at the time of writing she is laid up.

Then there is the *Misr*, which is not a paddle steamer, even though she looks like one—the paddle-wheel panels on her sides are just for show; she is a twin-screw steamer but she is authentically historic. Like the *Karim*, she was built for the British Admiralty during the First World War; she was sent directly to Egypt, where she arrived in September 1918 and was termed surplus to requirements, and sold to the Egyptian government. Her subsequent history is obscure until she was purchased and renovated in the 1990s by an independent tour operator and put at the service of Nile tourists.

As with the *Karim*, the operators of the *Misr* make claims she once belonged to and was used by Egyptian royalty, which may or may not be true,

---

★ There are also one or two original old boats at permanent moorings. What may be Cook & Son's *Delta* is reportedly still being used as a floating restaurant at Cairo, while a boat once called the *Mahasen*, which possibly dates back to 1908, is now the *Nile Peking*, a Chinese restaurant in the channel beside the island of Roda in Cairo.

but during the 1960s there was a genuine former royal yacht taking tourists up and down the Nile. She was the *Kassed Kheir*, a 237-foot sidewheel steamer, built in 1926 by Thornycroft of Southampton on the order of King Fu'ad I of Egypt. She looked not unlike a small Cook's steamer, but with ornate gold scrolling on the paddle boxes, bow, and stern. She had royal apartments on the main deck, and guest staterooms and a formal dining room on the upper deck. The observation lounge was decorated in the manner of a palm court, while next door, the drawing room was done out in Louis XV style. When Fu'ad died, the *Kassed Kheir* passed to his son and heir, Faruq, until he had to give her up, along with everything else, in the wake of the revolution. During the 1950s she served as a floating hotel, then a floating restaurant and casino, before she was purchased by local travel agency Eastmar in 1961 and refitted as a Nile cruise ship with accommodation for seventy. Sadly, she was destroyed by fire in the early 1970s.

The same moneyed clientele that supports the *Sudan* has also given rise to an equally delightful phenomenon, the revival of the *dahabiya*. The centuries-old Nile sailboat beloved of Amelia Edwards and other early Egyptian travelers has made a minor comeback. They first started appearing at the end of the 1990s; these were new boats but built to designs copied from old plans and vintage photographs. At the beginning of the twenty-first century there were just a handful of these vessels, but now there are as many as forty on the Nile, most available for hire. (Not all of the *dahabiya*s are employed in the tourist business; some are private houseboats. The Egyptologist Dr. Kent Weeks lived aboard his 85-foot-long *dahabiya*, the *Kingfisher*, moored close to the Mummification Museum at Luxor, from 2003 until 2013.) A few utilize original iron hulls salvaged from the river, but the tourist boats incorporate every comfort and convenience that might be demanded by the modern traveler accustomed to first-class cabins and executive lounges, from the choice of twenty-five Havana cigars in the library to mirrored glass windows for privacy. No need for rat traps these days.

Meanwhile, for any entrepreneurs whose sense of romance is second only to their ambition and tenacity, there are several rusting wrecks of old steamers dotting the banks of the Nile. There is the previously mentioned *Memnon*, lying in two parts in dry dock in Cairo, and also the Cook & Son's *Fostat*, and the former Anglo-American boats *Indiana* and *Niagara*. It may well be that all four of them are too far gone to be salvaged but, as with all journeys on the Nile, real and imagined, it's good to dream.

ABOVE AND OPPOSITE One of the new breed of *dahabiya*s. This boat, *Zekrayaat* (Arabic for "memories"), is based on an original design from the late 19th century, and is owned and operated by the Nile Dahabiya travel company

THE NILE FLEETS FROM AMASIS TO ZINAT AL-NIL

What follows is a listing and brief description of the boats that made up the Nile fleets of Thomas Cook & Son and the Anglo-American Nile Company. The Tewfikiya Nile Navigation Company and Express Nile Navigation Company both also had Nile fleets but I have been unable to discover anything about these beyond the names of those boats referred to in chapter seven.

THOMAS COOK & SON

Prior to 1886, when John Mason Cook set about developing his own fleet, the company leased boats from the khedive. Between 1869 and 1884, these included at various times the *Beherah* (berths for 45 passengers), *Benha*, *Beniswaif* (20), *Ghizeh*, *Jasrieh*, *Mahmoudieh* (17), *Masr* (54), *Mehallah* (36), *Nile* (24), and *Saidieh* (27).

Information on the fleet post-1886, when Cook & Son began building its own boats, is drawn mainly from the company's Nile brochures, which were issued annually, and from notices in *Cook's Excursionist* and *Travellers' Gazette*. When it comes to specifications for

The steamer *Amasis*, formerly the *Prince Mohammed Ali*

the boats, sources often disagree; I have gone with the figures at the time of construction.

Notes on the eventual fates of some of the boats come from a letter sent by Cook & Son's Cairo office in 1952 in response to a request for this information, and from a document compiled in 1966 by J.H. Price, editor of *Cook's European Timetable* from 1952–85. There is some conflict between the two and I have sided with the 1952 letter because its level of detail is more convincing. Both documents are part of the Thomas Cook Archive at Peterborough.

Amasis First-class paddle steamer, formerly the *Prince Mohammed Ali*; see page 171. She was commandeered by the British Army in December 1915 and sent to Mesopotamia, from where she never returned.

Ambigole Sternwheel steamer, leased by the British government to Cook & Son some time in the 1880s. She was returned to the British Army in 1896 for use in the campaign to retake Khartoum.

The 118-foot *dahabiya* *Ammon-Ra*, flying the Cook & Son ensign

Amenartas Paddle steamer, built in 1888 by J. McArthur Paisley of Clydeside, with engines by Bow McLachlan. She was introduced for use on the Express Service between Asyut and Aswan for the season 1888–89, with cabins for 40 passengers. She was commandeered by the British Army in December 1915 and never returned.
Length 140ft; breadth 25ft; draft 6ft 6ins; engine 400hp

Ammon-Ra *Dahabiya*, constructed at Cairo on a steel hull supplied from one of the Clydeside shipbuilders. She was introduced for the season 1890–91 and sold off in 1918.
Length 118ft; breadth 17ft 6ins

Amosis Paddle steamer, purchased from an unknown source in 1886, and refitted with new engines before being put into service for the season 1887–88. She was initially used on the Express Service between Asyut and Aswan but proved unsuitable and, after just one season, was downgraded to use as a tug.

Anubis Steam launch, built around 1890 and used for towing *dahabiya*s.

Arabia First-class paddle steamer, built in 1911 by John Thornycroft Ltd. of Southampton, Great Britain, at a cost of £39,227. She made her maiden Nile-service sailing on 21 November 1911 and operated between Cairo and Aswan, with cabins for 80 passengers. With the outbreak of the Second World War, she was moored opposite the British Club at Gezira, Cairo, and served as a floating officers' club and hostel. After the war she became a floating hotel. She was sold to Ahmed Bey Youssef al-Tawil in November 1949 but details after that are sketchy; she may have been sold to Misr Shipping, who chartered her out to local travel agents. More certain is that *Arabia* was beached at Rod al-Farag, just north of central Cairo, for a time in the early 1960s before being refitted for use once again as a static hotel and possibly operated by the Eastmar tourist company, first at Aswan, then later back in Cairo. In 1966, while under

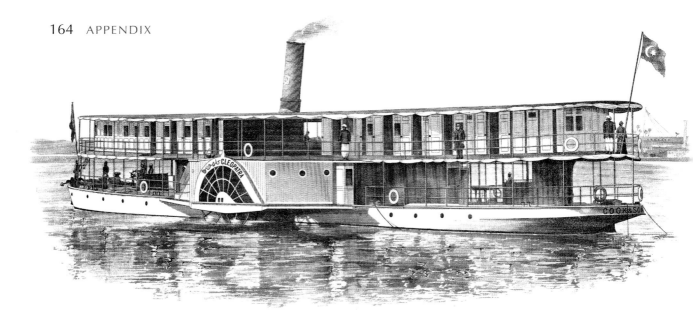

When introduced in 1888, the *Cleopatra* made the fastest sailing ever from Cairo to Aswan and back

charter to Hapi Tours, the *Arabia* caught fire at its mooring in front of the Semiramis hotel and was destroyed.

According to the minutes of the annual general meeting of Cook & Son (Egypt) Ltd for 1907, that year the company purchased a sternwheel steamer called *Arabia*: what happened to this boat and why its name was given to a new vessel four years later is a mystery.

Length 236ft; breadth 32ft (51ft over the paddles); draft 3ft 10ins; displacement 600 tons; engine 500hp

Attieh al-Rahman *Dahabiya*, introduced into the fleet for the season 1887–88.

Cheops *Dahabiya*, introduced into the fleet in the early 1890s and with cabins for seven passengers. She was sold off in 1935.
Length 106ft; breadth 17ft 3ins

Chonsu Paddle steamer, formerly the *Mena*; see page 168. A private steamer with cabins for 12 passengers that was in use until at

least the late 1930s; her fate thereafter is unknown.

There was a wooden-hulled *dahabiya* of the same name that was part of the fleet in the early 1890s.
Length 125ft; breadth 18ft; engine 130hp

Cleopatra Paddle steamer, built in 1888 by J. McArthur Paisley of Clydeside, with engines by Bow McLachlan. She was introduced for use on the Express Service between Asyut and Aswan for the season 1888–89, carrying 40 passengers. She was commandeered by the British Army in December 1915 and never returned.
Length 140ft; breadth 25ft; draft 6ft 2ins; engine 400hp

Damietta Sternwheel steamer, a refit of a paddle-wheel vessel originally meant for hospital duty on the Tigris in Mesopotamia. She entered service with Cook & Son in 1921 and was used primarily on the Express Service between Asyut and Aswan, with cabins for 60 passengers. She was sold to the British Army's Inland Water Transport department in 1942.

Length 231ft; breadth 32ft; draft 3ft 6ins; engine 500hp

Delta Sternwheel steamer, originally the *Luxor* before being lengthened and widened at Bulaq in 1924, and relaunched with a new name. She was distinguished by having a fourth deck, which served as an open-air sun deck. She was used on the Express Service between Asyut and Aswan, with cabins for 44 passengers. She was sold to His Excellency Ahmed Bey Ghaleb in October 1948; fate thereafter unknown.

Length 159ft; breadth 27ft; draft 3ft; engine 400hp

Egypt First-class paddle steamer, built in 1907 by John Thornycroft Ltd. of Southampton, Great Britain, at a cost of £35,437, although all woodwork and fittings, etc., were supplied by Cook & Son at the company works at Bulaq. She made her maiden Nile voyage in December 1907 and operated between Cairo and Aswan, with cabins for 80 passengers. She was sold to Gamal al-Din al-Abd Bey in March 1950; fate thereafter unknown.

Length 230ft; breadth 32ft (51ft over the paddles); draft 3ft 10ins; displacement 565 tons; engine 500hp

Fostat Small sternwheel steamer, built in 1907, with cabins for nine passengers; she was used as a private steamer for hire. She was sold to Madame Fardos Zulficar Bey in October 1948. In the early 1960s, she was purchased by the Oriental Institute of the University of Chicago to house members of an expedition involved in the Nubian Salvage Campaign, rescuing monuments from the rising waters created by the construction of the High Dam. The hull was remodeled and the engines removed to provide more living and working space, after which she had to be moved around by tugboats. She later served as a floating dig-house at Luxor, before

The *Egypt* was Cook & Son's first new paddle steamer of the twentieth century

being taken over by the American Research Center in Egypt, who moored her near the Giza Bridge at Cairo where she served as the director's residence. ARCE sold her in 1990 and, at the time of writing, she currently lies derelict on the banks of the Nile somewhere near Luxor.

There was also a *dahabiya* of the same name, purchased in 1891 and introduced to the fleet for the season 1891–92.
Length 114ft; breadth 18ft; draft 3ft; engine 185hp

Gazelle Cook & Son's smallest *dahabiya*, purchased in 1891 and introduced to the fleet for the season 1891–92.
Length 83ft; breadth 16ft

Hapi Steam launch, used as a tug for towing *dahabiya*s.

Hatasoo Paddle steamer, introduced for use on the Express Service between Asyut and Aswan for the season 1890–91, with cabins for 40 passengers. She was commandeered by the British Army in December 1915 and never returned.
Length 160ft; breadth 25ft; engine 400 hp

Hathor *Dahabiya*, constructed at Cairo on a steel hull supplied from one of the Clydeside shipbuilders and introduced for the season 1890–91. She was sold off in 1918.
Length 118ft; breadth 17ft 6ins

Herodotus *Dahabiya*, introduced into the fleet in the late 1880s/early 1890s.
Length 106ft; breadth 17ft 3ins

Horus *Dahabiya*, constructed at Cairo on a steel hull supplied from one of the Clydeside shipbuilders and introduced for the season 1889–90.
Length 108ft; breadth 17ft 6ins

Hyksos Small paddlesteamer, introduced into the fleet for the season 1910–11 and used for private hire.

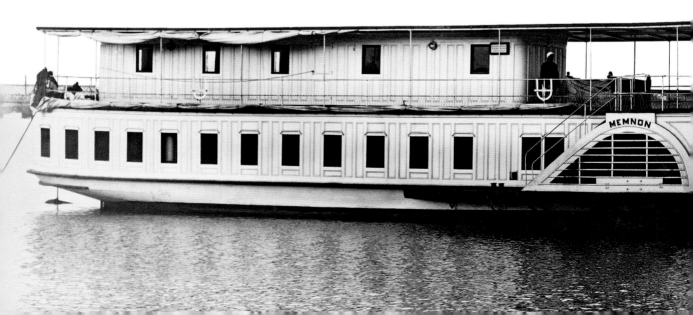

Ibis Sternwheel steamer, built by Fairfield Govan in 1885 for the British Army, who subsequently leased the vessel to Cook & Son. With cabins for 28, she was used on the service between the First and Second Cataracts until the British Army asked for her return in 1896 for use in the campaign to retake Khartoum. She was then acquired by the Sudanese government, who ran her between the First and Second Cataracts to connect with the scheduled rail services to Khartoum. In 1938 she was used in the film *The Four Feathers*, starring Ralph Richardson. She was reported to still be in existence as recently as 2004, but her current whereabouts are unknown.

Isis *Dahabiya*, constructed at Cairo on a steel hull supplied from one of the Clydeside shipbuilders and introduced for the season 1889–90.

Luxor Sternwheel steamer, purchased from an unknown source in 1912. In 1924, at the Bulaq shipyard, she was sawn lengthways and breadthways to be enlarged, and relaunched as the *Delta*; see page 165.

Maat *Dahabiya*, purchased in 1901; sold off in 1918.

Mansourah *Dahabiya*, purchased in 1889 and introduced for the season 1889–90.

Masr One of the old khedivial steamers that remained part of the Cook & Son fleet after the Sudan campaign but was possibly scrapped, sold, or returned to the government in the early 1890s.

Memnon A small steamer, built in 1903, with cabins for 19 passengers, used on the Second Cataract service between Aswan

The *Memnon* is the boat used in the 1978 cinema film of *Death on the Nile*

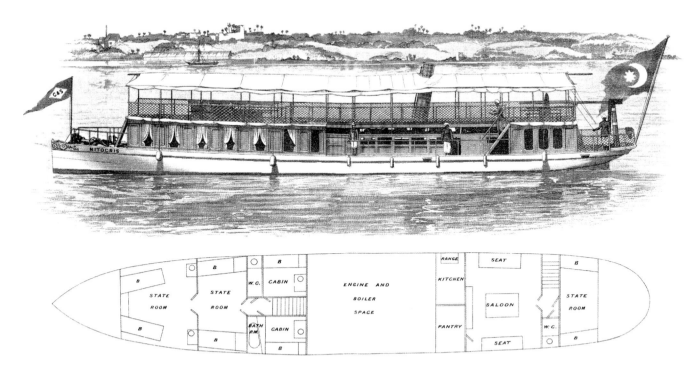

The *Nitocris* was almost unique in the Cook & Son fleet for being screw-driven rather than paddle wheels

and Wadi Halfa. She was replaced on this service by the *Thebes* for the 1912–13 season, after which she was switched to use as a private steamer for hire. She was sold to the four-time Egyptian prime minister Ali Maher Pasha in October 1948, who used her as a houseboat, and whose son later leased her, in 1960, to the Oriental Institute of the University of Chicago for use in the Nubian Salvage Campaign, rescuing monuments from the rising waters created by the construction of the High Dam. Apparently her engine hadn't been used in twelve years and all machinery had to be overhauled before the *Memnon* steamed under her own power from Cairo up to Nubia with the Institute's team aboard. She was later sold to a local tour operator, possibly Seti the First Travel, and maintained in working order.

She featured in the 1978, all-star film version of *Death on the Nile* masquerading as the *Karnak*. For a time, she served as a floating restaurant at Cairo but, at the time of writing, she is in dry dock in two halves after a plan to extend her was abandoned.
Length 131ft; breadth 19ft; draft 2ft 6ins; engine 150 hp

Mena Small paddle steamer, built in 1890 with cabins for ten passengers. She was rebuilt in 1911 and renamed the *Chonsu*; see page 164.
Length 100ft; breadth 18ft; draft 3ft; engine 120hp

Menes Paddle steamer, part of the fleet in the late 1880s and 1890s, an old boat used for towing *dahabiya*s.

Nefertari Paddle steamer, built in 1888 by J. McArthur Paisley of Clydeside, with engines by Bow McLachlan. She was introduced for use on the Express Service between Asyut and Aswan for the season 1888–89, carrying 40 passengers. She was commandeered by the British Army in December 1915 and never returned.
Length 140ft; breadth 25ft; draft 6.5ft; engine 400hp

Nepthis *Dahabiya*, constructed at Cairo on a steel hull supplied from one of the Clydeside shipbuilders and introduced for the season 1890–91. She was sold off in 1918.
Length 118ft; breadth 17ft 6ins

New Star *Dahabiya*, purchased in 1891.

Nigma Standard wooden-hulled *dahabiya* that was added to the Cook & Son fleet some time before 1888.

Nitocris Bought from an unknown source and introduced into the fleet in 1887 for use as a "steam *dahabiya*"—a private steamer suitable for small parties of up to eight. Unlike the other boats in the fleet, the *Nitocris* was not a paddle steamer but had twin screws. She was sold to a private buyer, Mr. Rene Zarb, in August 1941, for use as a houseboat. Zarb was later arrested as a spy during the era of President Nasser and the boat impounded; fate thereafter unknown.
Length 103ft; breadth 15ft; draft 3ft 3ins; engine 80hp

Oonas A small paddle steamer, built in 1898 and entering service that year. She had nine cabins accommodating 11 passengers, plus a stateroom, dining salon, and smoking room. She was sold to a private buyer in 1939 and according to J.H. Price rebuilt around 1960 and chartered out; fate thereafter unknown.
Length 110ft; breadth 18ft; draft 2ft 3ins; engine 130hp

Osiris Steel-hulled *dahabiya*, constructed at Cairo on a hull supplied from one of the Clydeside shipbuilders and introduced for

Oonas was one of several small steamers used for private hires

the season 1889–90. She was sold off in 1918. *Length 108ft; breadth 17ft 6ins*

Pepi Paddle steamer, purchased from sources unknown in 1886, and refitted, including new engines, before being put into service for the season 1887–88. She was initially used on the Express Service between Asyut and Aswan but proved unsuitable and, after one season, was put to use as a private steamer for hire and, later, as a tug.

Philites Standard wooden-hulled *dahabiya*, added to the Cook & Son fleet some time before 1888.

Prince Abbas First-class paddle steamer, with hull, engines, and superstructure built in 1886 by Fairfield Govan of Clydeside, Scotland, and shipped in sections to Cairo where she was put together. She made her maiden Nile-service voyage on 30 November 1886. Initially, she ran between Cairo and Aswan, but after 1896, being a smaller boat, with cabins for only 44 passengers, she was switched to the less-trafficked Second Cataract service between Aswan and Wadi Halfa. She was overhauled and redecked in 1905, before being commandeered by the British Army in December 1915 and sailed to Mesopotamia, from where she never returned, fate unknown.

Confusingly, there was a second ship built in Scotland just a few years later also called the *Prince Abbas*. Trialed in March 1892, this vessel was a 2,000-ton screw steamer commissioned by the Egyptian government and intended to be operated by the Khedivial Steam Packet Service as a fast mail and passenger service between Alexandria, Athens, and Constantinople. It was considerably bigger than the Cook boat with a length of 300ft. This ship was also requisitioned and saw service during the First World War at Gallipoli, where she was

As Cook & Son's biggest boat during the company's Nile heyday, it is possible that more tourists sailed on the *Rameses* than on any other boat in the fleet

commended for performing good service under fire during the landings of Allied troops in April 1915; she was also involved in the evacuation in December 1915 and January 1916. She was sold in 1916 to the Hudson Bay Company and torpedoed and sunk by a U-boat in the North Sea in 1917.

There is also a modern vessel named the *Prince Abbas*; built in 1998 in a heritage style, she carries 130 guests in 60 cabins, is owned and operated by the Mövenpick Group, and sails on Lake Nasser.
Length 160ft; breadth 20ft; draft 7.2ft; engine 300hp

Prince Mohammed Ali First-class paddle steamer, with hull, engines, and superstructure built in 1886 by an unknown French shipyard on the Rhône, and then towed across the Mediterranean and down the Nile to Cairo, where she was fitted out. Her maiden Nile-service voyage was in January 1887, and she operated between Cairo and Aswan, with cabins for 44 passengers. In the summer of 1901 she was modified and renamed *Amasis*: see page 162.
Length 160ft; breadth 20ft; draft 7.2ft; engine 350hp

Ptah Steam launch, used for towing.

Rameses First-class paddle steamer, with hull, engines, and superstructure built in 1886 by an unknown shipyard on the Rhône, originally for the French government, which canceled the order. Instead, she was bought by Cook & Son, who had her towed across the Mediterranean and down the Nile to Cairo, where she was fitted out.

She was configured with 25 double-berth cabins and 20 single, to accommodate 70 passengers (later this went up to 79). She made her maiden Nile-service voyage in January 1887, operating between Cairo and Aswan. For 24 years she was the largest vessel in the fleet (after 1911 she had to share the honor with the *Arabia*). She was commandeered by the British Army in December 1915 with the intent of being sent to Mesopotamia, but was destroyed by fire at Bulaq in January 1916 just as refitting was being completed.
Length 236ft; breadth 30ft; draft 2ft 6ins; engine 500hp

Rameses the Great First-class paddle steamer, with hull, engines, and superstructure built in 1889 by Fairfield Govan of Clydeside, Scotland, and shipped in sections to Cairo where the boat was put together. She made her maiden Nile-service voyage on 4 February 1890, and operated between Cairo and Aswan, with accommodation for 80 passengers. She was commandeered by the British Army in December 1915 with the intent of being sent to Mesopotamia, but was destroyed by fire at Bulaq in January 1916 just as refitting was being completed.
Length 221ft; breadth 30ft; draft 2ft 6ins; engine 500hp

Rameses the Third First-class paddle steamer, with hull and superstructure built in 1892 by J. McArthur Paisley of Clydeside, Scotland, and shipped in sections to Cairo where the boat was put together. She made her maiden Nile voyage on 17 January 1893, and operated between Cairo and Aswan,

Serapis, slightly bigger sister vessel to the *Oonas*

with accommodation for 70 passengers. She was commandeered by the British Army in December 1915 for service in Mesopotamia and, while there, was destroyed by fire at Amara on the River Tigris.
Length 200ft; breadth 28ft; engine 500hp

Rosetta Sternwheel steamer, this was a refit of a paddle-wheel vessel originally meant for hospital duty on the Tigris in Mesopotamia, which entered service with Cook & Son in 1921. She was used primarily on the Express Service between Asyut and Aswan, with accommodation for 60 passengers. She was sold to the British Army's Inland Water Transport department in 1942.
Length 225ft; breadth 30ft; draft 3ft 6ins; engine 500hp

Scarab Sternwheel steamer, purchased in 1905, this was a small steamer for private hire, with accommodation for six passengers. She was sold to a private buyer in February 1939; fate thereafter unknown.
Length 90ft; breadth 17ft; draft 2ft; engine 90hp

Sebek Steam launch, built around 1887–89.

Serapis Paddle steamer, built in 1900 and entering service that year. She was a small, private steamer with 10 cabins for 15 passengers, plus two staterooms, a dining salon, and smoking room. She was sold to a private buyer in February 1939; fate thereafter unknown.
Length 125ft; breadth 18ft; draft 2ft 6ins; engine 130hp

Sesotris *Dahabiya*, added to the fleet in the late 1880s/early 1890s. Sold off in 1934.
Length 106ft; breadth 17ft 3ins

Sethi Sternwheel steamer, bought in 1886 and added to the fleet for the season 1887–88. She operated on the Second Cataract service until her engines were removed in 1893 and put into the *Rameses the Third*, after which she was moored at Aswan for use as a floating hotel, accommodating up to 30 guests; this arrangement lasted for two or three seasons, after which her fate is unknown.

Seti Paddle steamer, bought by Cook & Son in 1910 as the *Melika* and renamed; she was used as a private steamer for hire, with accommodation for eight passengers. She was sold to a private buyer in February 1939; fate thereafter unknown.
Length 100ft; breadth 18ft; draft 2ft 6ins; engine 120hp

Sroura *Dahabiya*, part of the fleet in the late 1880s.

Sudan First-class paddle steamer, for which the order was placed with Bow McLachlan & Company of Paisley, Scotland, in 1914 or earlier; however, construction was halted by the outbreak of the First World War. The hull was delivered to Egypt by 1918 but the engines and boilers were put on hold. It was not until 8 February 1921 that the *Sudan* made her maiden Nile-service voyage; thereafter she operated alongside sister ships *Arabia* and *Egypt* on the Cairo–Aswan service. She had accommodations for 80 passengers. During the Second World War she was moored at Cairo and used as an officers' club. In March 1950, she was sold to Fuad Serageldin, secretary-general of Egypt's Wafd Party and holder of various pre-revolution cabinet posts, but she was taken from him a few years later under the nationalization process. She subsequently found her way into the possession of the Egyptian-owned Eastmar Line and was put back to work carrying tourists. At some later date she was taken on by the French tourism company Club Méditerranée, who moored her at Luxor

Original drawing of the *Sudan* by Bow McLachlan engineers

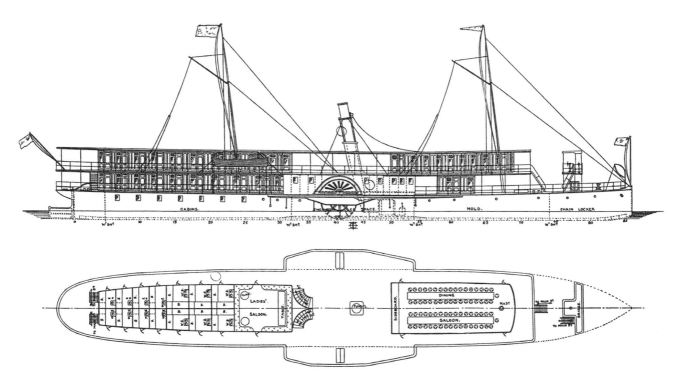

as a floating hotel but kept her in working order with a Scottish engineer who would steam her and undertake a short run every so often. Since 2003 she has been owned by the French travel company Voyageurs du Monde, who operate her ten months of the year on weekly sailings between Luxor and Aswan. The *Sudan* appeared as the *Karnak* in the 2004 British TV film of *Death on the Nile*, starring David Suchet as Inspector Poirot, which was shot almost entirely on location in Egypt.

According to the minutes of the annual general meeting of Cook & Son (Egypt) Ltd for 1907, that year the company purchased a sternwheel steamer called *Sudan*: what happened to this boat is a mystery.
Length 236ft; breadth 32ft (51 feet over the paddles); draft 3ft 10ins, displacement 600 tons; engine 500hp

Sultana *Dahabiya*, purchased in 1891 and added to the fleet for the season 1891–92.

Tahta Paddle steamer, purchased in 1890–91, an old boat used for towing *dahabiya*s.

Tewfik First-class paddle steamer, with hull, engines, and superstructure built in 1886 by Fairfield Govan of Clydeside, Scotland, and shipped in sections to Cairo, where she was put together. She made her maiden Nile-service voyage on 15 November 1886 and initially operated between Cairo and Aswan, but being a smaller boat, accommodating only 44 passengers, she was later switched to the less-trafficked Second Cataract service between Aswan and Wadi Halfa. She was overhauled and redecked in 1905,

but was destroyed by fire in Egypt while being prepared for British Army service in Mesopotamia in January 1916.
Length 160ft; breadth 20ft; draft 7ft; engine 300hp

Thames *Dahabiya*, a relatively small vessel, with cabins for only four passengers. Sold off in 1934.
Length 93ft 9ins; breadth 16ft 3ins

Thebes Sternwheel steamer, bought in 1912 and used on the Second Cataract service between Aswan and Wadi Halfa, with accommodation for 48 passengers. She was sold to the Sudanese government in 1948; fate thereafter unknown.
Length 150ft; breadth 26ft; draft 3ft 6ins; engine 300hp

Thosco Twin-screw motor launch, built 1934. She had no cabins and was used only for day excursions.
Length 50ft; breadth 14ft; engine 180hp

Thotmes Paddle steamer, entered into service in 1887, as a refitted and remodeled older boat. She was initially employed on the Express Service between Asyut and Aswan but proved unsuitable and, after one, season was downgraded to use as a tug.

Tih *Dahabiya*, built in the late 1880s.

Toski Sternwheel steamer, leased by the British government to Cook & Son in the 1880s. The British Army took her back in 1896 for use in the campaign to retake Khartoum.

The *Thebes* getting up steam before leaving her moorings

Zinat al-Nil *Dahabiya*, configured to carry only six passengers. She was sold off in 1935.
Length 112ft; breadth 17ft 9ins

ANGLO-AMERICAN NILE COMPANY

Unlike Cook & Son, precious little record of the Anglo-American Company survives today. There is no company archive, and even the basic facts such as when exactly the company was founded, by whom, and when it was dissolved remain unknown. (History may be written by victors, but it is also slanted toward those who maintain the best archives.) Information on the boats is similarly scarce, but these steamers were all part of the fleet at one time or another, although not necessarily coexisting.

Britannia First-class sternwheel steamer, which seems to have been a later vessel, added to the fleet around 1915. She was used on the Cairo–Aswan service, with cabins for 63 passengers. She remained in service at least until the end of the 1940s but after this her fate remains unknown.
Length 200ft; breadth 28ft; engine 500hp

Columbia Small twin-screw steamer, built in 1896 as a boat for private charter with cabins for 10 to 14 passengers.
Length 110ft; breadth 16ft; draft 2ft 6ins; engine 400hp

Germania First-class sternwheel steamer, introduced for the 1905–1906 season. She was used on the Cairo–Aswan service with accommodation for 66 passengers. She was added to the fleet soon after Anglo-American

amalgamated with the transatlantic Hamburg America Line; after the two companies parted the *Germania* no longer appears as part of the Nile fleet.
Length 200ft; breadth 28ft; engine 600hp

Indiana Small sternwheel steamer, built in 1897. She was used on the Second Cataract service with accommodation for 16 passengers. During the First World War she served as a hospital boat on the Suez Canal, but afterward returned to Nile passenger service until the end of the 1940s. She was reportedly used for many years for river maintenance and had a spell as a houseboat moored at Cairo. She now lies derelict in a creek near the island of Roda in Cairo.
Length 120ft; breadth 19ft; draft 2ft; engine 300hp

Mayflower First-class sternwheel steamer, built at the Anglo-American Company works at Bulaq in 1897. She made her maiden voyage on 3 January 1898. She was used on the Cairo–Aswan service with accommodation for 50 passengers. She remained in service at least until the Second World War, after which she was, for a time, a floating hotel, used to accommodate passengers on flying-boat services transiting through Cairo; her fate thereafter remains unknown.
Length 180ft; breadth 26ft; draft 2ft; engine 500hp

Niagara Small sternwheel steamer, built in 1896 as a boat for private hire, with cabins for 10 passengers. During the First World War she served as a hospital boat on the Suez Canal, afterward returning to passenger service

until the end of the 1940s. In 2011, she was photographed moored on the Nile in Cairo, but in a dilapidated condition.

Length 110ft; breadth 19ft; draft 2ft; engine 300hp

Nubia First-class sternwheel steamer, introduced for the 1905–1906 season. She was used on the Cairo–Aswan service, with cabins for 42 passengers. As with the *Britannia*, the *Nubia* arrived following the amalgamation with the transatlantic Hamburg America Line and also disappeared from the Nile fleet after the partnership was dissolved.

Length 160ft; breadth 25ft; engine 400hp

Puritan First-class sternwheel steamer, built for Anglo-American in Scotland in 1898; her maiden Nile voyage was in January 1899. She was used on the Cairo–Aswan service, with cabins for 80 passengers. She remained in service at least until the Second World War, after which, like the *Mayflower*,

she was for a time a floating hotel used to accommodate passengers on flying-boat services transiting through Cairo; her fate thereafter remains unknown.

Length 200ft; breadth 28ft; draft 2ft; engine 600hp

Victoria First-class sternwheel steamer, built for Anglo-American in Scotland in 1899; her maiden Nile voyage was in January 1900. She was used on the Cairo–Aswan service, with cabins for 72 passengers. She remained in service at least until the end of the 1940s, but after this her fate remains unknown.

Length 200ft; breadth 28ft; draft 2ft; engine 600hp

Less attractive than the Cook & Son boats, the Anglo-American fleet, which included the *Puritan*, was designed to sit high in the water and reduce the risk of running aground

SELECT BIBLIOGRAPHY & SOURCES

In addition to the titles listed below, an invaluable reference were the brochures promoting the company's Egypt & Nile business issued annually by Thomas Cook & Son from the late 1880s through until the 1930s, as well as the volumes of *Cook's Excursionist* and *Travellers' Gazette*, and sundry other letters and documents, all part of the extensive and fascinating Thomas Cook Archive at Peterborough maintained by the ever amenable Paul Smith.

Richard Hill was a former civil servant in Sudan, who in the late 1960s began making notes for a book he planned to call *Tourists on the Nile*; the book was never finished but his papers, held in the Sudan Archive at the University of Durham, were of help, particularly regarding the earliest Nile steamers. The National Archives at Kew provided information on the requisition of Nile steamers by the British Army for use in Mesopotamia during the First World War and on the British Foreign Office's support for Thomas Cook & Son in Egypt after the Second World War.

Bartlett, William Henry. *The Nile Boat, or Glimpses of the Land of Egypt*. London: Arthur Hall, Virtue & Co, 1849.

Bell, Lilian. *As Seen by Me.* New York: Harper and Bros., 1900.

Bell, Reverend Charles D. *A Winter on the Nile, in Egypt, and in Nubia*. London: Hodder and Stoughton, 1888.

Beresford, Charles. *The Memoirs of Admiral Lord Charles Beresford*. Boston: Little, Brown, & Company, 1914.

Brendon, Piers. *Thomas Cook: 150 Years of Popular Tourism*. London: Secker & Warburg, 1991.

Brocklehurst, Marianne. *Miss Brocklehurst on the Nile: Diary of a Victorian Traveller in Egypt*. U.K.: Millrace, 2004.

Budge, Sir E.A. Wallis. *By Nile and Tigris: A Narrative of Journeys in Egypt and Mesopotamia on Behalf of the British Museum Between the Years 1886 and 1913*. London: John Murray, 1920.

Burns, Reverend Jabez. *Tourist Helpbook for Travellers to the East: Egypt, Palestine, Turkey, Greece and Italy*. London: Thomas Cook, 1872.

Butler, Colonel Sir William Francis. *The Campaign of the Cataracts: Being a Personal Narrative of the Great Nile Expedition of 1884–5*. London: Sampson Low, Marston, Searle & Rivington, 1887.

Caillard, Mabel. *A Lifetime in Egypt*. London: Grant Richards, 1935.

Cameron, Roderick. *My Travel's History*. London: Hamish Hamilton, 1950.

Carey, M.L.M. *Four Months in a Dahabëéh, or Narrative of a Winter's Cruise on the Nile*. London: L. Booth, 1863.

Carson, Blanche Mabury. *From Cairo to the Cataract*. Boston: L.C. Page & Co., 1909.

Christie, Agatha. *Death on the Nile*. London: Collins Crime Club, 1937.

De Guerville, Amédée Baillot. *New Egypt*. London: William Heinemann, 1905.

Doyle, Arthur Conan. *The Tragedy of the Korosko*. London: Smith, Elder, & Co., 1898.

Ebers, Georg. *Egypt: Descriptive, Historical, and Picturesque*. London: Cassell & Company, Limited, 1887.

Edwards, Amelia B. *A Thousand Miles up the Nile*. London: Longmans, Green, & Co., 1877.

Etzensberger, Robert. *Up the Nile by Steam*. London: Thomas Cook & Son, 1872.

Gaschke, Jenny. *Edward Lear: Egyptian Sketches.* London: National Maritime Museum, 2009.

Hibbert, Christopher. *Edward VII: The Last Victorian King.* London: Viking, 1976.

Hill, Richard. *Sudan Transport: A History of Railway, Marine and River Services in the Republic of the Sudan.* London: Oxford University Press, 1965.

Humphreys, Andrew. *Grand Hotels of Egypt in the Golden Age of Travel.* Cairo and New York: The American University in Cairo Press, 2011.

Joanne, Adolphe, and Isambert, Emile. *Itinéraire de l'Orient.* Paris: Librarie de L. Hachette et Compagnie, 1861.

Marden, Philip Sanford. *Egyptian Days.* Boston and New York: Houghton Mifflin Company, 1912.

Marlowe, John. *The Making of the Suez Canal.* London: The Cresset Press, 1964.

Morgan, Janet. *Agatha Christie: A Biography.* London: Collins, 1984.

Prime, William Cowper. *Boat Life in Egypt and Nubia.* New York: Harper & Brothers, 1874.

Pudney, John. *The Thomas Cook Story.* London: Michael Joseph, 1953.

Reid, Donald Malcolm. *Whose Pharaohs? Archaeology, Museums, and Egyptian National Identity from Napoleon to World War I.* Berkeley: University of California Press, 2002.

Robins, Nick. *The Coming of the Comet: The Rise and Fall of the Paddle Steamer.* Barnsley: Seaforth Publishing, 2012.

Romer, Isabella. *A Pilgrimage to the Temples and Tombs of Egypt, Nubia, and Palestine in 1845–46.* London: Richard Bentley, 1846.

Russell, William Howard. *A Diary in the East during the Tour of the Prince and Princess of Wales.* London: George Routledge and Sons, 1869.

Sayce, Reverend Archibald Henry. *Reminiscences.* London: Macmillan and Co., 1923.

Sladen, Douglas. *Egypt and the English.* London: Hurst and Blackett Limited, 1908.
———. *Queer Things about Egypt.* London: Hurst and Blackett Limited, 1911.

Steevens, George Warrington. *Egypt in 1898.* New York: Dodd, Mead & Company, 1899.

Swinglehurst, Edmund. *The Romantic Journey: The Story of Thomas Cook and Victorian Travel.* London: Pica Editions, 1974.

Tirard, Helen Mary, and Nestor Tirard. *Sketches from a Nile Steamer: For the Use of Travellers in Egypt.* London: Kegan Paul, Trench, Trübner & Co. Ltd., 1891.

Twigger, Robert. *The Red Nile.* London: Weidenfeld & Nicholson, 2013.

Warburton, Eliot. *The Crescent and the Cross: or, Romance and Realities of Eastern Travel.* New York: Wiley and Putnam, 1845.

Warner, Charles Dudley. *My Winter on the Nile.* Boston: Houghton, Mifflin and Company, 1881.

Wheatley, George W. *The Oriental Pocket Companion: A New Guide for Travellers to India, China &c, by the Overland Route, via Egypt, embracing Southampton, Marseilles, Trieste, and Constantinople Lines, and the New Steam Route from Cairo to Thebes.* London: G. W. Wheatley & Co., 1852.

Wilbour, Charles Edwin. *Travels in Egypt: December 1880 to May 1891.* New York: Brooklyn Museum, 1936.

Wilkinson, Toby. *The Nile.* London: Bloomsbury, 2014.

Withey, Lynne. *Grand Tours and Cook's Tours: A History of Leisure Travel 1750 to 1915.* New York: William Morrow and Co., 1997.

INDEX

ILLUSTRATION CREDITS

All photographs and illustrations are from the collection of the author with the exception of the following: Galleria L'Image, original vintage posters, Alassio, Italy: 1, 52, 53, 54, 126, 133, 134, 149; Cornelius von Pilgrim, Swiss Institute, Cairo: 2–3, 124; Thomas Cook Archives: 12, 13, 14, 15, 46, 50, 51, 56–57, 64, 82, 85, 86–87, 88, 89, 90–91, 92–93, 94, 95, 96, 98, 99, 100, 101, 103, 104, 108, 109 (top), 110, 111, 113 (right), 114, 115, 116 (top), 117, 118–19, 121, 127, 129, 130–31, 132, 136–37, 138, 140, 143, 146–47, 156, 162, 163, 164, 165, 166–67, 168, 169, 170, 172, 174, 177; Shafik Gabr Collection: 29; Library of Congress: 37; Getty Research Institute: 40–41; Corbis Images: 62, 125; TopFoto: 102, 122, 142; National Archives, Kew: 135; The Christie Archive: 145; András Zboray of www.fjexpedition.com: 151; Voyageurs du Monde (www.voyageursdumonde.fr): 152, 158, 159; Poole Flying Boat Celebration: 155; Liss Fine Art (www.lissfineart.com): 157; Ayman Simman of Nile Dahabiya Boats (www.nile-dahabiya.com): 160, 161; Bow, McLachlan & Co. Ltd. archive, University of Glasgow: 173.

ACKNOWLEDGMENTS

This book would absolutely not have been possible without the cooperation of Paul Smith, who presides over the Thomas Cook archive at the company headquarters in Peterborough, England. I owe a great debt to him for making available to me the vast amounts of documents, ephemera, and photographs that sit in his care, and for frequently directing my attention to items I might have overlooked. Thank you, Paul.

Thank you also to Susan Allen for recollections of the *Fostat* and for sharing her enthusiasm for Nile steamers; Doris Behrens-Abouseif for information on the origins of *dahabiya*s; Alessandro Bellenda of Galleria L'Image, Alassio, Italy, for allowing us to reproduce posters from his personal collection; Fabien Cazenave of Voyageurs du Monde, present owners of the *Sudan*; Alistair Deayton and Alan Dumelow for leads on surviving Nile steamers, and, in Alan's case, sharing his research on the *Kassed Kheir*; Anne and Harry Masterton-Smith for first-hand recollections of Cook & Son operations in Egypt in the 1960s and 1970s; Michael Phipp for sharing the photograph of the flying boat at Cairo; Cornelius von Pilgrim for images of steamers at Aswan; Kathleen Sheppard for documents on Egyptologists and their Nile boats; Ayman Simman of Nile Dahabiyas for the inside story of the *dahabiya* revival; Gilbert Sinoué for more stories about the *Kassed Kheir*; and Kent Weeks for entertaining ideas and theories.

Massive thanks, as ever, to my collaborator and partner in this project, Gadi Farfour.

For more about Egypt in the golden age of travel, visit www.grandhotelsegypt.com